Nashtaneer,
Malancha

THREE WOMEN

In this series

Durgeshnandini—Bankim Chandra Chattopadhyay

Nashtaneer, Dui Bon,
Malancha
THREE WOMEN

....

Rabindranath
TAGORE

....

Translated by
ARUNAVA SINHA

RANDOM HOUSE INDIA

boipatra

Published by Random House India in 2010
1

Translation © Arunava Sinha 2010
Introduction © Shirshendu Chakraborti 2010

Random House Publishers India Private Limited
MindMill Corporate Tower, 2nd Floor, Plot No 24A
Sector 16A, Noida 201301, UP

Random House Group Limited
20 Vauxhall Bridge Road
London SW1V 2SA
United Kingdom

978 81 8400 1327

Typeset by SwaRadha Typesetting, New Delhi-91

Printed and bound in India by Replika Press Pvt. Ltd.

Contents

Introduction

Between *Nashtaneer* (1901) and *Dui Bon* (1933) or *Malancha* (1934), there is a gap of more than three decades and the reader may find it rather odd that they have been included for translation in a cluster. While there are obvious differences between the early and later works of Tagore, these are perhaps less important than the central preoccupation, if not obsession, that unites them: an anatomy of upper-class conjugal relationship, in particular, women's problematic location in it. On the one hand, trauma and loneliness in the home pushes the women to the brink of hysteric madness where they discover their unknown sexual intensities. On the other hand, the same women may imprison themselves in stereotypes of domesticity. Needless to say, such themes and issues are absent in many of Tagore's earlier short stories with a rural background. As he puts it in a discussion late in his career, while the early stories had a youthful freshness, tenderness, and spontaneity, his later fiction, focusing on urban life, was marked by psychological complexity and a conscious use of technique (*Forward*, 23 February, 1936). This urban fiction is characterized by an almost banal, everyday family life involving sober financial planning and calculation: the male protagonists are all engaged in business. The placid surface is then suddenly broken up by a seismic upheaval equally in matters of the heart and those of finance. Financial fraud and collapse accompany emotional treachery and turmoil.

The paradigm of transgressive, often self-destructive, passion of women within a patrician or middle-class milieu can of course be traced back to the domestic fiction of Bankim Chandra Chatterjee. Barring a few exceptions, the Victorian domestic novel had been marked by settled family life and the prudential distrust of ungovernable passion. Thus, it could not have served as a model for Bankim or Tagore. At the same time, Victorian values were a visible 'civilizing/colonizing' influence on the Bengali middle and upper classes, shaping the ideals of companionate marriage, family, and home. But if Victorian morality gave rise to a new concept of domesticity, Tagore's fictional representation of it exposed the stifling hypocrisy and limitations of that morality. Victorian values may have introduced the notion of companionate marriage to the middle-class Hindu household, but the entire process involved a poeticization of women. Thus, a prosaic and routine domesticity is turned into a sanctimonious ideal by a rhetoric of mystification. Tagore formulates his critique of the process in many of his writings: in *Ghare Baire* (1916), for instance, he does this appropriately through the interior monologue of Bimala, the heroine. Recalling her mother's role as devoted wife, she simultaneously realizes that the unaffected, self-effacing simplicity of that domestic routine is beyond recovery. She discovers that the humdrum domesticity of the immediate past was being supplanted by a poeticized and mystified version, public opinion now responded to change by moulding

> that which was as easy as breathing into a poetic art. The imaginatively inclined men of today are raising their pitch constantly as they hold forth on the unparalleled poetry of the wifely devotion of married women and abstinence of widows. It is evident from this how in this domain of life there has been a breach between truth and beauty (*Rabindra Rachanabali*, vol. 4, Vishwabharati, 1987, p. 474; translation mine).

Sharmila (*Dui Bon*) and Niraja (*Malancha*) are victims of this mystification.

The couples in these three novellas and indeed in most of Tagore's urban fiction are childless. While it is common knowledge that a barren wife or one producing only girls was held in contempt—even the memoirs of Jnanadanandini Devi, wife of one of Tagore's elder brothers, bear witness to this attitude—such issues are kept out by Tagore. Moreover, the mother-in-law or sister-in-law is conspicuously absent in the novellas. Evidently, Tagore excludes these relatives here in order to concentrate on the man–woman relationship which is specifically under stress in a period of transition. But the childlessness is more puzzling, especially in view of the unprecedented importance of childhood in his entire oeuvre, including critical and educational writings. The obvious contrast here is with the domestic fiction of Sarat Chandra Chatterjee where much of the happiness of the family derives from children. Could childlessness then be seen as a conscious strategy to question the inauthenticity ('breach between truth and beauty') of the domestic ideal discussed above?

Sharmila's maternal solicitude for her husband, juxtaposed with her childlessness, may thus indicate a mismatched relationship. As Tagore had put it in a letter, Shashanka and Sharmila had never really been united, although the cracks were not visible on the surface. Their marital relationship is therefore like a make-believe game and Shashanka openly rebukes her for treating him like a toy in front of the world. Despite her suffering, Sharmila somewhat masochistically surrenders to the stereotype of the woman who is ruthlessly left at home by her husband in pursuit of his commercial enterprise which for her is the eternal masculine, heroic struggle with fate. Her younger sister, Urmimala, is very different, impulsive, curious, and brimming over with vitality. But Nirad wishes to dominate her completely, disguising his love of power and money in the form of lofty ideals according to which he would mould her nature like a scientific procedure in the laboratory. Urmi submits to this subtle tyranny, this aestheticization, much against her nature, although fortunately she is not trapped into marriage. Internalizing the sermons of Nirad, she would periodically chastize herself and adopt an ascetic regimen even when he was away in Europe. She thus finds release from this stifling priggishness in the light-hearted relationship with Shashanka bordering upon adultery.

Niraja's love is also possessive, relentlessly directed equally at the garden, the pet dog, and the dependant's son. After the dog's sudden death, when her own child dies during delivery, she is physically shattered and never recovers from it. But even on her sickbed, with the knowledge of impending death, she is unable to give up her exclusive claim on the garden. The case of Charulata (*Nashtaneer*) is somewhat different. Here Tagore hints at a sexual and emotional denial on the part of the husband who is so absorbed with publishing an English newspaper that he initially does not notice, and when his attention is drawn to the fact, does not understand Charu's growth from a child-bride to a young woman.

Childlessness could also be seen as a metaphor that prefigures the decline of the aristocratic classes. In Tagore's social and political writings, there is a premonition of this doom and its bearing on his own class status, but he came to terms with it rather early and endorsed social transformation. Nikhilesh, the zamindar in *Ghare Baire*, openly associates Bharatvarsha with the lower castes and Gora searches the soul of India not among the elite but among the toiling masses. We may also recall that despite doubts about totalitarianism inherent in communism, Tagore was inspired by the emancipation of the common people in Russia which he saw in 1930, a few years before he wrote the two later novellas.

Perhaps this sense of a devitalized aristocracy is captured in the mysterious onset of disease in these two novellas. However, the metaphor is more than social and is brutally psychological, exposing the inability of middle-class men and women, trapped in codes of decency, to acknowledge the biological drives behind any love relationship. Niraja discovers that her marital relationship with Aditya has been rendered hollow and her mind rendered petty and harsh by her loss of strength and beauty; the living world around her, which ironically comes to her deathbed in all its sensuousness, has little time for her bloodless, dying form. In the very first chapter, we learn that her lonely afternoons are marked by time signals as she looks at the quiet garden she loves and beyond it into emptiness receding into emptiness. There is a similar inevitability in Sharmila's undiagnosed illness—from which she recovers unlike her brother, Hemanta—which brings Urmi to Shashanka and catalyzes the growth of adulterous passion.

Love between man and woman, when dismantled of its rhetoric, reveals an inescapable element of mutual possessiveness. Expressing itself in solicitude and concern, love can conceal a desire to dominate or control. In the ultimate analysis, this possessiveness presupposes the ego's attachment to worldly possessions. Perhaps that is why in *Malancha*, objects take on a life of their own, suggesting Niraja's jealousy-driven possessiveness. Ramen's advice to Niraja is to acquire freedom from being tormented by her husband's relationship with Sarala by giving up all her claims. As long as you think your wealth is being snatched away by someone, there is no respite from agony; but once you give up your most precious possession for the sake of the one you love the most, you experience happiness and peace.

If the only freedom is the freedom from possessive desire and if such desire is the necessary pre-condition of love, if the desire to dominate is interchangeable with the desire to be dominated, then what is the way out of this impasse? As Nikhilesh had realized in *Ghare Baire*, 'the day I can really release the bird from its cage I will realize that it is the bird who releases me. The one I bind in a cage binds me in my desire and that is bondage stronger than that of chains' (552). Responding to the envious interrogation of Niraja, Aditya describes his love for Sarala as the product of growing up wild together in the forest shade, oblivious of each other's existence. By contrast, their conjugal relationship approximates a punctilious ritual—as Aditya puts it, it was Niraja and not Sarala who aroused poetic feelings in him. Sarala's beauty was irrelevant to Aditya's love for her since he knew Sarala simply as Sarala. In accordance with such an equal relationship, Sarala affirms that Aditya is as much a dependant of her as she is of him. This realization, reminiscent of Nikhilesh's insight, is echoed a few pages later by Aditya when he asks himself whether he had given refuge to Sarala or Sarala had given him refuge.

In all the three novellas, the characters do not understand each other and indeed themselves fully. Bhupati and Charu, for instance, move in virtually two parallel conversational corridors without a meeting point. Amal, as a budding writer, proficient in a florid style of Bengali is unable to grasp the force of Charu's literary style praised by the critics. Above all, Amal cannot quite follow the deeper meaning of Charu's teasing, playful talk, her attitude to Manda and reaction to Amal's public recognition as an author. She is thus trapped in her own language which no one around her really understands. Charu reconciles herself to a double life in which she fulfils her duties as wife while constructing a subterranean existence around sorrow at separation from Amal. But that most secret, interior, cherished space where she is herself sans disguise and mask has no place for anyone else—even Amal's presence is in the form of a cherished memory, an absence.

The language of *Nashtaneer* is firmly grounded in the realistic tradition and whatever interiority there is, is described unsentimentally and economically from the outside. In the later two novellas, particularly in *Malancha*, Tagore attempts to foreground interiority and capture the intricate and intersecting movements of the consciousness in an appropriately fine-spun style. This is why the characters converse as though in a reverie befitting a poem or poetic drama. The resulting style performs several functions at the same time. The same style enables Ramen to hide himself and his emotions in idle elegant talk and express his reflections on life without making them ponderous. The crafted prose is not without its counterpoint in the speech of servants, thereby hinting at the somewhat enclosed world of upper-class women and men. While the servants have their passions too, they do not aspire to a refined mastery of them. By contrast, the class position of Tagore's heroines goads them towards concealing their passions and maintaining the decorum of polite society. In such a social situation, the poetic prose can serve the function of hiding or covering, thereby suggesting the repressed energies underneath. The hallucinatory language creates a claustrophobic atmosphere which heightens the loneliness of the women and brings out the stress underlying tranquil family life. It thus serves throughout in its conscious artistry as a foil to the unconscious, a veneer over the repressed passions that often explode with overwhelming force.

The instability is evident in Niraja's dying outburst, in the uncontrolled sobbing of Charu or in the vehement remorse of Urmi, but it is equally conveyed by the warped maternal solicitude of Sharmila. Caught up in the cross-purpose conversation and hallucinatory poetry, the reader is drawn out of the habitual and familiar range of responses to recognize the fault-lines of settled domesticity and sympathize with the somewhat hysteric tenor of women's private lives. By contrast, the men lack in emotional intensity and are pampered by society into emotional immaturity, they cannot really share in their wives' destinies. Thus the lonely, traumatized women of Tagore are nevertheless given a space of their own, where they can reflect upon and come to terms with their situation in life. In this sense, Tagore remains a feminist before his time.

Shirshendu Chakrabarti is Professor of English at Delhi University and a published poet and critic in Bengali.

Nashtaneer (1901)

The Broken Nest

Neither of them noticed that the period in which husband and wife rediscover each other in the exquisite first light of love had slipped silently into the past. Even before savouring the new, they had become old, familiar and accustomed to each other.

One

BHUPATI HAD NO need to work. He had enough money, and, moreover, the land was too hot. But the stars at his birth had made him an industrious man. This was why he felt compelled to publish an English newspaper. Now he no longer had to grumble about time hanging heavy on his hands.

Since childhood, he had had a penchant for writing and making speeches in English. He would write letters to English newspapers even when there was no reason to; he never missed a chance to speak up at public gatherings even when he had nothing to say. Politicians wooing him for his wealth had heaped lavish praise upon him for his compositions, and this had given him a high opinion of his proficiency in the language.

Umapati, Bhupati's brother-in-law and a lawyer—eventually abandoning his attempt to run his legal practice—told his sister's husband, 'Why don't you publish an English newspaper, Bhupati? Considering your incredible...' etcetera.

Bhupati was stirred. There was no glory in having one's letters published in someone else's newspaper; in his own, he would be able to wield his pen with complete freedom. Appointing his brother-in-law as his assistant, Bhupati thus ascended the editor's throne at a rather early age.

The passion for journalism and the passion for politics are both powerful in youth—and there were plenty of people to ensure that Bhupati became besotted.

While he remained thus engrossed with his newspaper, his child bride Charulata matured into young womanhood. The newspaper editor missed this important news entirely. His attention was concentrated on the unrestrained expansion of the government's frontier policy.

Living as she did in a wealthy household, Charulata had no chores to do. The only task of her long, undemanding days and nights was to blossom fruitlessly, rather like the flower that will never ripen. In such circumstances, wives go to great excesses over their husbands if they can—with the game of married life shifting its boundaries from the defined and the conventional to the chaotic and the anarchic. Charulata did not have this opportunity. Piercing the armour of the newspaper to claim her husband proved to be a difficult task.

One day, after a female relative had chided him, drawing his attention to his young wife, Bhupati told himself in a moment of self-awareness, 'That's true, Charu needs a companion, the poor thing has nothing to occupy her all day.'

He told his brother-in-law Umapati, 'Why don't you send for your wife, Charu has no one of her age to talk to, she must be very lonely.' Mandakini, his brother-in-law's wife, was settled in his home; Mr Editor was relieved having diagnosed the absence of female company as the cause of Charu's misery.

Neither of them noticed that the period in which husband and wife rediscover each other in the exquisite first light of love—that gold-tinged dawn of conjugal life—had slipped silently into the past. Even before savouring the new, they had become old, familiar, and accustomed to each other.

Charulata had a natural propensity for reading and so her days did not prove unbearably heavy. She had made her own arrangements for books. Bhupati's cousin—his paternal aunt's son—was a third year college student; Charulata turned to him for help with getting her books to read. In return for this service, she had to accede to many of Amal's demands. She was frequently made to finance his meals at restaurants and the purchase of English literary works. Amal would have his friends over for meals sometimes; Charulata would make all the arrangements and thus pay for her tuition. Bhupati may have made no demands of Charulata but, in return for some meagre help with her reading, there was no end to cousin Amal's requirements. Charulata feigned rage over them now and then, but it had become necessary to prove herself useful to someone and endure the happy oppression of affection.

'The son-in-law of the owners of our college comes to Footnore classes in velvet slippers specially made for him, bouthan*,' said Amal, 'I simply cannot bear it any more. I have to have a pair of velvet slippers, or else my standing will suffer.'

Charu: Indeed! As if I shall slave away to make a pair of slippers for you! Here's some money—go buy yourself a pair.

'Not a chance,' said Amal.

Charu neither knew how to make slippers, nor did she want to confess as much to Amal. But no one besides Amal ever demanded anything of her, and she could not resist fulfilling the prayer of the one person in the world who sought something from her. Secretly—and meticulously—she began to learn the art of making velvet slippers while Amal was away in college. When Amal himself had completely forgotten his orders, Charu sent him an invitation to dinner.

As it was summer, a seat had been prepared on the terrace for Amal's meal. The plate was covered with a brass lid, lest dust get into the food. Shedding his college garb, Amal washed and dressed before making an appearance. Sitting down, he removed the lid—to discover a newly made pair of wool slippers on the plate! Charulata laughed aloud.

---

*Traditional form of address for ones brother's (or cousin's) wife.

The shoes stoked Amal's expectations. Now he wanted a high-necked coat, next a silk handkerchief with floral patterns had to be made for him, after that an embroidered cover became essential for the oil-stained armchair in his sitting room.

Each time, Charulata refused, causing an argument, and each time, she tenderly surrendered to Amal's whims. Sometimes Amal asked, 'How far have you got, bouthan?' 'Barely started,' she would lie. Sometimes she would say, 'I didn't even remember.'

But Amal wouldn't give up. He would remind her every day and maintain his steady chorus of demands. Charu would feign indifference, goading Amal into a state of agitation—and then unexpectedly fulfil his wishes, savouring his response.

In this affluent household Charu did not have to do anything for anyone, barring Amal, who never rested without making her do something for him. These small labours of love kept her heart alive and fulfilled.

To dub the plot of land that lay behind Bhupati's house a garden would be an exaggeration. The primary vegetation of this so-called garden was an ambarella* tree.

Charu and Amal had set up a committee for the development of this plot. Together they had conjured up the garden of their dreams with diagrams and plans.

'Bouthan, you must water the plants in our garden yourself like the princesses of yore,' said Amal.

'And we'll have a hut there in the western corner for a fawn,' added Charu.

'We'll have a small pond too, with ducks in it,' contributed Amal.

---

*The word used in the Bengali text is 'bileti aamra', that is, the English aamra, a relatively uncommon fruit today. It is not to be confused with the more ubiquitous aamra, a sour fruit used mainly to make pickles and chutneys.

Excited by the idea, Charu responded, 'And I'll have some blue lotuses in there, I've always wanted to see the blue lotus.'

'We'll have a little bridge over the pond,' suggested Amal, 'with a tiny boat at its bank.'

'The bank will be paved with white marble, though,' Charu told him.

Amal drew a map of the garden with great ceremony, using paper and pencil, ruler and compass. Together they drew up some two dozen maps, recreating their vision each day.

After the map was finalized, they proceeded to estimate expenses. Initially the plan was that Charu would use some of her monthly stipend to build the garden gradually; Bhupati never spared a glance for anything that went on at home, when the garden was ready they would give him a big surprise. He would think they had used Alladin's lamp to transplant an entire garden from Japan.

Yet, no matter how much they lowered their estimates, Charu could not afford the expense. Amal set out to modify the map yet again. 'Let's leave the pond out in that case, bouthan,' he said.

'No, we simply can't, that's meant for my blue lotus,' Charu protested.

'Why not do away with the tiled roof for your fawn's hut; a thatched roof will do just as well,' Amal suggested.

'Never mind, I don't need the hut in that case,' said Charu, furiously.

The plan was to get seeds of cloves from Mauritius, of sandalwood from Karnat, and of cinnamon from Ceylon, but when Amal proposed replacing them with seeds of everyday Indian and English plant from the local market, Charu looked glum. 'Then I don't want a garden,' she said. This was not the way to lower expenses. It was impossible for Charu to curb her imagination alongside the estimate, and no matter what he said, it wasn't acceptable to Amal either.

'Then, bouthan, you'd better discuss the garden with dada—he's certain to give you money for it.'

'You and I will make the garden together. There's no fun if I tell him. He might just order an Eden Garden from some English gardener—where will our plan be then?'

In the shade of the ambarella tree, Charu and Amal indulged themselves over their impossible scheme. Charu's sister-in-law Manda called out from the first floor 'What are you two doing in the garden at this hour?'

'Looking for ripe ambarella,' answered Charu.

'Bring me some too, if you find any,' said Manda, greedily.

Charu smiled. So did Amal. The great pleasure and glory of all their schemes was that it was limited to just themselves. Whatever other qualities Manda might possess, imagination wasn't among them; how would she savour ideas like these? She was thus always excluded from any committee that had these two as its members.

The estimate for the impossible garden didn't shrink; nor did the imagination yield an inch. Amal identified the spots in the garden meant for the pond, for the hut, for the fawn, for the marble platform.

He was using a small spade to mark out the area around the plum tree that would have to be paved in their dream garden when Charu remarked, 'How wonderful it would be if you were a writer, Amal.'

'Why would it be wonderful?' asked Amal.

'I'd have made you write a story with a description of this garden of ours. This pond, this fawn's hut, this ambarella tree… they'd all be in it, but no one except us would understand, what fun. Why don't you try to write, Amal, I'm sure you can.'

'Very well, what will you give me if I can write?' asked Amal.

'What do you want?' enquired Charu.

'I'm going to sketch the pattern of a vine on the roof of my mosquito net; you'll have to embroider it in silk.'

'Must you overdo everything? Fancy having an embroidered mosquito net!'

Amal orated eloquently against the practice of relegating the mosquito net to the status of a graceless prison. It only proved, he argued, that ninety per cent of people in the world had no appreciation of beauty, and did not find ugliness the least bit painful.

Charu accepted this argument at once, and was happy to conclude that 'our secret two-member committee does not belong to that ninety per cent'.

'All right, if you write, I'll embroider your mosquito net,' she agreed.

'You think I can't?' asked Amal mysteriously.

'Then you must have written something already, show me,' Charu exclaimed.

Amal: Not today, bouthan.

Charu: No, you must show me today—I beg of you, fetch it now.

It was Amal's extreme eagerness to read what he had written to Charu that had held him back all this time. What if Charu didn't understand it, what if she didn't like it—he had been unable to shed his apprehensions. Today, he drew out his notebook, blushed a little, cleared his throat, and then began to read. Leaning back against the trunk of the tree, her legs stretched out on the grass, Charu listened.

The subject of the essay was 'My Notebook'. Amal had written, 'O my alabaster notebook, my imagination is yet to leave its mark on thee. Thou art as pure, as unfathomable, as the brow of the newborn ere the messenger of fate doth enter the chamber of birth. Where now is that hour when I shall write the conclusion to the last verse and chapter on the last page? Thy tender infant ivory leaves cannot even

9

dream this day of that ink-stained termination… ' and a great deal more.

Charu listened in silence in the shade of the tree. When Amal had finished reading, she said after a brief silence, 'And you claim you cannot write!'

Amal sipped the heady brew of literature for the first time that day under the tree—the wine-bearer was young, the taste was fresh—while the late afternoon light deepened into long shadows.

'We must pick some fruit for Manda, Amal,' said Charu 'What's our excuse if we dont?'

Since they were not inclined to tell Manda about their discussions, they were forced to pick fruit for her.

Two

NEITHER AMAL NOR Charu noticed that their dream of creating a garden had dissolved, like so many other such schemes, somewhere in the depths of their imagination.

Amal's writing now became the principal subject of their discussions. 'Bouthan, I feel this splendid notion coming upon me,' Amal might say.

'Come on over to the south verandah—Manda will be here any minute with her paan,' Charu would respond eagerly.

She occupied a worn wicker chair in the verandah, built in the Kashmiri style, while Amal sprawled on the high ledge of the railing.

The subjects of Amal's essays were seldom well defined. It was difficult to explain them clearly and beyond anyone's means to comprehend what he tried to say in his muddled way. 'I can't explain to you properly, bouthan,' Amal himself would acknowledge, repeatedly.

'No, I've understood a good deal,' Charu would tell him. 'Write it down now, don't put it off.'

She would understand some of it, find the rest incomprehensible; drawn by the fire of Amal's expression, she would fill the gaps with her imagination. This was enough to make her happy, as well as impatient for more.

'How far have you written?' Charu would ask the very same evening.

'Do you expect me to finish it in a day?' Amal would ask her.

'You haven't even written it yet,' Charu would grumble.

'Wait, I have to think about it a little more,' Amal would tell her.

'Go away then!' Charu would say angrily.

Her rage would mount by evening. Just when a furious Charu would be ready to stop talking to Amal he would, under the pretext of taking his handkerchief out of his pocket, allow her to catch a glimpse of a wad of paper he had scribbled on.

Charu's vow of silence would be shattered immediately. 'There! You *have* written it. You think you can fool me? Show me!'

'It's not done yet,' Amal would answer. 'I want to write a little more before reading it to you.'

Charu: No, you have to read it this instant.

Amal was dying to read it to her immediately; but not before allowing Charu to grab at it once or twice. Then, taking a seat, he would first arrange the sheets, make a correction here or there with his pencil—Charu's eager anticipation hanging heavily over the sheaf of papers all the while like rain-bearing clouds.

Whenever Amal wrote two or three paragraphs, however little it may have been, he had to read them out to Charu instantly. The rest of it would then be composed through discussion. All this time they had been engaged in building castles in the air; now they lost themselves in the construction of verses.

One afternoon, Amal returned from his college with his pocket unusually full. As he stepped inside the house, Charu observed the weight in his pocket from a window. Usually when he was back from college, Amal wasted no time going into the women's chambers, but today he dawdled in the drawing room, his pockets full, showing no inclination towards going inside.

Charu clapped her hands several times from the periphery of her chambers but no one responded. In a fit of mild rage, she

12

marched off to her verandah, holding a book by Manmatha Datta and attempted to read it.

Manmatha Datta was a new author. His style was rather similar to Amal's, which was why Amal never had anything good to say about him; from time to time he would read out Datta's essays to Charulata, mocking him by distorting his pronunciation. Snatching the book out of Amal's hands, Charu would toss it aside contemptuously.

When she heard Amal's footsteps that afternoon, Charu raised the selfsame Manmatha Datta's book, titled *Chorus*, to her face, reading it with great concentration.

She pretended not to notice Amal entering the verandah. 'Well, bouthan, what are you reading?' enquired Amal. Receiving no answer, Amal circled around Charu's chair to take a look at the book. '*Bogus*, by Manmatha Datta,' he commented.

'Don't disturb me, please,' said Charu, 'let me read.' Standing behind her, Amal began to read, mockingly, 'I am a blade of grass, an insignificant blade of grass. O tree, my friend in crimson regal dress, I am but a blade of grass. I offer no flower, no shade, I cannot raise my head heavenwards, in spring the cuckoo cannot enchant the world from the shelter of my leafy canopy—but still, O tree my friend, do not ignore me from your flower-bedecked boughs; I may only be a blade of grass by your feet, still do not humiliate me.'

Having read thus far, Amal made up the rest, in jest: 'I am a banana, an unripe unloved banana, O pumpkin my friend, you who thatch roofs so beautifully, I am a mere banana.'

Charu's curiosity wouldn't allow her to continue her show of anger; laughing, she threw her book away, saying, 'You're so jealous, you don't like anyone else's writing but your own.'

'And you're so generous,' countered Amal, 'you want to trample over even an insignificant blade of grass.'

Charu: All right sir, enough of your wit. Show me what you have in your pocket.

Amal: Why not hazard a guess?

Continuing to tease Charu for a while, Amal finally extracted from his pocket a copy of the well-known magazine *The Lake Lotus*. Charu discovered that 'My Notebook', the essay that Amal had written earlier, had been published in it.

She fell silent. Amal had expected her to be delighted but when he saw no signs of any such pleasure, he commented, 'They don't publish any old piece in *The Lake Lotus*, you know.' Here Amal was guilty of exaggeration. The editor never turned down a piece if it was even passable. But Amal convinced Charu that the editor was in fact exceptionally demanding, approving barely one out of a hundred submissions.

Charu tried to force herself to feel happy but could not. She tried to understand why she felt so betrayed, but was unable to find any reason. Amal's writing belonged to her as much as to him. Amal was the writer and Charu, the reader. The secrecy of their venture was its primary attraction for her. She could not clearly comprehend why she should feel so upset at the thought of other people reading those pieces and praising them.

But the writer's ambition cannot be restricted to a single reader for long. Amal began to publish his pieces. Praise came his way too. He even started receiving letters from acolytes which he showed his sister-in-law. They caused Charu both pleasure and pain. Her enthusiasm and encouragement no longer remained the only things that could inspire him to write. Now and then, Amal even received anonymous letters from women. Charu would banter with him over them but without deriving any joy from this. The readers of Bengal had breached the doors of their committee and raised a barrier between them.

14

One day, in a rare moment of leisure, Bhupati told his wife, 'Indeed, Charu, I had no idea our Amal is such a clever writer.'

Bhupati's praise pleased Charu. She felt proud because her husband had acknowledged that though Amal was his dependant, he was different from others of his age. She wore an air that suggested, 'Now you know why I am so fond of Amal; I realized his true worth a long time ago, he does not deserve to be ignored.'

'Have you read his pieces?' Charu asked.

'Yes... no, not exactly,' answered Bhupati. 'I haven't had the time. But Nishikanta was praising him sky-high—he's a connoisseur of Bengali writing.'

Charu was extremely keen that Bhupati should hold Amal in high respect.

Three

Umapada was trying to persuade Bhupati to distribute free gifts with his newspaper. Bhupati simply could not comprehend how these gifts would convert his losses into profits.

Charu entered but left as soon as she saw Umapada in there. Returning some time later, she found the two still engaged in debate. Noting that Charu seemed impatient, Umapada left on some pretext while Bhupati continued to wrack his brains over the accounts.

'Aren't you done yet?' Charu asked on entering. 'How do you manage to devote all day to that paper of yours?'

Pushing his accounts aside, Bhupati smiled. 'Indeed, I never find the time to pay attention to Charu,' he told himself. 'This is unfair. The poor thing has nothing to do all day.'

'No studies today?' Bhupati asked her affectionately. 'Has your teacher escaped? Your school is truly contrary—the student is ready with her books, the master's missing. It seems to me Amal no longer tutors you as regularly as he used to.'

'Should Amal be wasting his time tutoring me?' asked Charu. 'Do you consider him an ordinary private tutor?'

Putting his arm around her waist and drawing her to himself, Bhupati said, 'Do you call this ordinary tutoring? If I had a sister-in-law like you to teach…'

Charu: Oh stop. Even as my husband you have no time, never mind someone else.

A trifle injured, Bhupati said, 'Very well, I promise to teach you tomorrow onwards. Fetch your books, let me take a look at them.'

Charu: Enough, you needn't teach me. For now, could you deign to put aside your newspaper accounts? Tell me if you can turn your attention to something else.

'I most certainly can. My attention will now be diverted to whatever you would have it diverted to.'

Charu: Very well, then, read this piece of Amal's—you'll see how wonderful it is. The editor has written to Amal to inform him that Nabagopal-babu has dubbed him Bengal's Ruskin after reading it.'

After this revelation Bhupati accepted the magazine with a degree of trepidation. Opening it, he read the title, 'The Monsoon Moon'.

Bhupati had been turning large numbers over in his head for the past two weeks in connection with the Indian Government's Annual Budget; he was not quite prepared at the moment to read 'The Monsoon Moon' from start to finish. Nor was the essay particularly short.

It began thus. 'Why doth the monsoon moon play hide-and-seek among the clouds all night? As though she hath purloined something from heaven, as though she hath nowhere to hide her blemish. When there hath been not a speck of a cloud in the spring sky, she hath presented herself brazenly in the naked sky to the eyes of the world—but today her voluptuous smile—akin to the infant's dream, to the remembrance of a lover, to the pearl necklace that dangles like the forelocks of the heavenly lord's consort doth…'

'Elegantly written,' observed Bhupati, scratching his head. 'But why me? I cannot appreciate such poetry.'

'What can you appreciate then?' responded Charu defensively, snatching the magazine from Bhupati's hands.

'I'm a man of the world, I appreciate people,' said Bhupati.

17

'Doesn't literature talk of people?' asked Charu.

Bhupati: They get it wrong. Besides, when you have flesh-and-blood people, why do you need to look for them in made-up stories?

'For instance, I appreciate you,' he continued, cupping her chin in his hand, 'but do I have to read the poem for that?'

Bhupati was proud of not being able to understand poetry. But even without having read Amal properly, he harboured a feeling of respect for him. 'To be able to spout words so effortlessly even without having anything to say is a skill that I could never master, no matter how hard I tried. Who'd have known Amal had such hidden talents?'

Although Bhupati acknowledged himself as a man without a taste for art, he was no miser when it came to literature. If a poor writer were to ask him for help, Bhupati gave him the money to publish his book only being very particular to warn him 'not to dedicate the book to me'. He used to purchase every weekly and monthly Bengali magazine, big or small, and every book, well known or unknown, readable or unreadable. 'I do not read books—if I do not buy them either, I will be sinning without atonement.' Because he did not read, he did not abhor indifferent writing in the least, which was why his library was full of Bengali books.

Amal used to assist Bhupati at proofreading; he entered with a sheaf of papers to show him some indecipherable writing in one of the articles.

'Write as much as you like about monsoon moons and autumn palms, Amal,' said Bhupati smiling. 'I have no objection—I do not wish to interfere with anyone's independence why interfere with mine? Your sister-in-law won't be satisfied till I've read it all—what kind of torture is this?'

'Indeed, bouthan,' Amal said laughing, 'had I known you were going to use my pieces as a new way to intimidate dada, I would never have written them.'

Amal was unhappy with Charu for having shown his essays, which he had crafted with his heart and soul, to Bhupati who, having no inclination for literature, was making light of them. Realizing as much, Charu was upset. To change the subject she told Bhupati, 'Why don't you find a match for this brother of yours—his writing won't torment you any more.'

'Today's young men aren't as devoid of practical sense as we were. They're poetic in their imagination but astute in practice. You haven't been able to persuade your brother-in-law to get married, have you?' answered Bhupati.

After Charu had left, Bhupati told Amal, 'I'm caught up with this newspaper all the time, Amal, poor Charu is quite lonely. She has little to do, she wanders into my study sometimes. But my hands are tied. It would be wonderful if you kept her gainfully occupied with some reading and studying. If you can translate English poetry for her sometimes, she'd both benefit from it and enjoy it. Charu has quite a taste for literature.'

'She does,' agreed Amal. 'If bouthan read a little more I believe she could be quite a good writer too.'

'That would be expecting too much,' Bhupati smiled, 'but Charu is far more discerning about Bengali literature than I am.'

Amal: She has the power of imagination which is rare among women.

Bhupati: Among men too, of which I am prime evidence. All right, if you can mould your sister-in-law in some way, I will reward you.

Amal: How?

Bhupati: I will find a companion for your sister-in-law.

Amal: And then I'll have to mould her too. Is this how my life will be spent?

Modern young men, both of them—they never baulked at saying what came to their mind.

Four

GAINING A REPUTATION among readers had given Amal a new confidence. As meek as a schoolboy earlier, he now seemed to have become a celebrated man of letters. He was invited to read literary essays at conferences; editors and their heralds waited for him in his room seeking the opportunity to be his host at banquets; requests to attend and chair meetings flowed his way; even his stature among the servants and maids in Bhupati's home shot up.

All this time, Mandakini had not considered Amal a significant figure. Dismissing Amal and Charu's light-hearted exchanges as juvenile, she had busied herself with housework and preparing her paan; she considered herself superior to them and essential to the larger world.

Amal was a voracious consumer of paan; as Mandakini was in charge of preparing it, his overindulgence usually annoyed her. Conspiring to raid Manda's store of paan every now and then was one of many sources of laughter for Charu and Amal—but the misdeeds of these two capricious thieves did not amuse Manda in the least.

The truth is that no dependant looks favourably upon another. Manda found the additional housework on Amal's account humiliating. Because Charu favoured Amal, Manda could not say anything explicitly but she studiously ignored his needs. Nor did she ever give up the chance to launch a barb or two at him; the servants and maids joined in too.

Manda was thus a little surprised to witness Amal's ascent. This was not the same Amal. His gentle diffidence had vanished as though he now had the right to be contemptuous of others.

The man who wears his status confidently, who has acquired a certain power, can attract women easily. When Manda saw Amal, his head held high, command this new respect, she slowly began to look up to him as well. Charmed by his newfound glory, she saw the glow of his young face with fresh eyes.

Stealing her paan was no longer necessary. Amal's fame led to this other loss for Charu; their bond of conspiracy was snapped. The paan soon arrived on its own, Amal never had to ask.

Besides the pleasure they had once got out of the tricks they played to exclude Mandakini from their little cabal was all but ruined. It became difficult to keep her at a distance; she didn't like the idea that Charu was Amal's only friend, the only connoisseur of his work. She was ready to pay Charu back for all the earlier humiliation, with interest. So whenever Amal and Charu were together, Manda found a pretext to come between them, casting forth her shadow like the moon eclipsing the sun. Charu did not even get the chance to laugh over this change in Manda, as she was always present.

Needless to say, this intrusion on Manda's part did not infuriate Amal as much as it did Charu. He felt a quickening at this volte face on the part of a woman who had once been quite aloof.

But when Charu, upon spotting Manda from a distance, would say—softly but cuttingly—'There she comes,' Amal would join in with, 'Indeed, how annoying.' It was a ritual on their part to express irritation at the company of anyone else in the world; how could Amal suddenly give that up? When Mandakini finally approached, Amal would say, as though forcing himself to be polite, 'Well then, Manda-bouthan, is your paan still being stolen?'

Manda: Why do you have to steal what you can get any time?

Amal: It's more fun that way.

Manda: Carry on reading, why did you stop? I love listening.

Manda had shown no desire in the past for acquiring a reputation as a lover of oral literature. But 'as the times, so the manners'.

Charu didn't want Amal to read to Manda the philistine but Amal wanted her to hear him read his piece.

Charu: Amal has written a criticism of *Kamalakanta's Secretariat**, can it possibly be of any interest to you?

Manda: Maybe I'm uneducated, but do you think everything goes over my head?

Amal remembered a different encounter. Charu and Manda were playing cards when he had entered holding his piece. Impatient to read it to Charu, he was annoyed because they wouldn't stop playing. Eventually he announced, 'You'd better go on playing then, bouthan, I'll go read it to Akhil-babu.'

'Where do you think you're going?,' said Charu, clutching his shirt. She lost the game quickly to wind it up.

'Is it time for reading now?' said Manda. 'I'm off then.'

'Why don't you listen too?' said Charu, feigning politeness.

Manda: Spare me, I don't understand any of that nonsense; it just puts me to sleep.

She left, annoyed with both of them at having brought the card game to a premature end.

---

*Kamalakanter Daptar (1875)—A well known satire by Bankim Chandra Chattopadhyay.

That very same Manda was today eager to listen to a criticism of Kamalakanta. 'That's excellent, Manda-bouthan, I'm very fortunate to have you as a listener,' said Amal. Turning back the pages, he prepared to start again from the beginning; the first paragraphs were particularly replete with feeling, and he did not want to omit them.

'You'd promised to bring those old magazines from the library, thakurpo*,' Charu interjected quickly.

Amal: But not today, surely.

Charu: But of course it was today. Have you forgotten?

Amal: Why should I forget? You said…

Charu: All right then, don't get them. Carry on reading, I'll send Paresh to the library.

She rose to her feet.

Amal sensed danger. Manda understood and her mind turned against Charu at once. As Amal hesitated after Charu's departure, she said with a faint smile, 'Run after her, Charu's angry. You'll be in trouble if you read to me.'

It was virtually impossible for Amal to leave after this. Furious with Charu, he said, 'What do you mean trouble?', and made as if to read.

Covering his papers with both her hands, Manda said, 'No need, don't read.'

Holding back her tears, she left.

*Traditional way in which a married woman addresses her husband's younger brother (or male cousin).

Five

CHARU HAD BEEN invited out. Manda was plaiting her hair at home. Amal entered, the word 'bouthan' on his lips. Manda, knowing Amal was not unaware of Charu's engagement, said smiling, 'Poor Amal-babu, you were expecting someone else, not me. Such is your fate.'

'The bale of hay on the left is no different from the one on the right—equally inviting to the ass,' Amal countered and settled down.

Amal: Tell me about your home, Manda-bouthan, the village where you live.

Amal now listened to people with great interest in a bid to gather material for his writing. This was why he no longer ignored Manda as completely as he once had. Manda's way of thinking, her past, were all subjects of enquiry for him now. He proceeded to interrogate her closely; about where she had been born, what her village was like, how she had spent her childhood, when she had got married and so on. Nobody had ever expressed so much interest in her brief life. Manda rambled on happily, occasionally saying, 'All this probably makes no sense.'

'No, I'm enjoying this, do go on,' Amal encouraged her. Manda was in the middle of her story about a farmhand of her father's who was blind in one eye. He would occasionally go on an angry fast after quarrelling with his second wife. Forced by hunger to come back home and steal a bite, he had been caught by her. Amal was listening with rapt attention and laughing in amusement when Charu entered.

The thread of the story was snapped and Charu understood clearly that her arrival had interrupted a pleasant session.

'You're back early, aren't you, bouthan?' asked Amal.

'So I see,' said Charu. 'Far too early.' She made as if to leave again.

'I'm glad you're here,' said Amal. 'I was wondering how late you'd be. I've brought you Manmatha Datta's new book, *The Evening Bird* to read.'

Charu: Not now, I have things to do.

Amal: Your wish is my command, I shall do them all for you.

Charu had known Amal would buy a book today to read to her; to make him jealous she had planned to praise Manmatha Datta profusely so that Amal would mock his work, parodying it as he read it out. Having conjured up the scenes in her head, she had left the engagement early on the pretext of sickness, her mounting impatience making her ignore all requests to stay. Now she said to herself, 'I was enjoying myself there, it was wrong of me to come away.'

Manda was no less brazen. There she was, alone with Amal in the room, grinning shamelessly. What would people say if they were to chance upon them? But it was very difficult for Charu to rebuke Manda about this. Suppose Manda cited Charu's example in response? But their cases were quite different. She encouraged Amal to write, discussed literature with him—but Manda's intention was nothing of the sort. She was clearly weaving her web to trap this innocent young man.

It was Charu's duty to deliver the poor boy from this impending danger. But how was she to enlighten Amal about this temptress's motives—suppose the enlightenment did not curb the temptation but only enhanced it? Most unfair.

My poor brother. There he is slaving away at my husband's newspaper all the time, and to think Manda is perched on the corner of the bed plotting to entice Amal. Dada is unperturbed, he trusts Manda implicitly. How could she possibly stay calm after being witness to such activities?

But Amal was a changed man. Ever since he had begun writing and had acquired a reputation, things had been going wrong. It was Charu who had sparked his writing career; she must have chosen an ill-fated moment to encourage him to write. For she could no longer assert herself with him as she was wont to earlier. Now that he had had a taste of acclaim from more than one person, it would make no difference to him if one of these people were to go away.

Charu concluded, with startling clarity, that Amal's passage from her exclusive patronage to that of myriad others could only spell imminent danger for him. He no longer considered Charu his equal; he had overtaken her. He was now a writer, and Charu, only a reader. This would have to be rectified.

Poor, simple Amal, poor temptress Manda, poor dada*.

---

*Elder brother.

Six

THE SKY WAS full of fresh monsoon clouds. Darkness had gathered inside the room and Charu was hunched near the open window, writing.

Not realizing that Amal had padded in silently to stand behind her, she kept writing in the soft light filtering in through the clouds, while Amal kept reading. One or two of Amal's published pieces lay open beside her; to Charu they were the only possible models of writing.

'And I thought you said you could not write!'

Charu was startled by Amal's voice; swiftly concealing her notebook, she said, 'Not fair.'

Amal: Why isn't it fair?

Charu: Why were you spying on me?

Amal: Because I cannot look openly.

Charu made as if to tear up her sheets. Amal snatched the notebook out of her hand.

'If you read it I'll never talk to you again in my life,' threatened Charu.

Amal: If you forbid me I'll never talk to you again in my life.

Charu: For my sake, thakurpo, don't read it.

Eventually Charu had to admit defeat. After all, she had been dying to show Amal what she had written; though she had not imagined she would be so self-conscious when it actually came down to it. When Amal finally began reading, after much coaxing and cajoling, Charu froze with embarrassment.

'I'll go get some paan,' she said, departing on the pretext of getting the ingredients for the paan.

When he had finished reading, Amal told Charu, 'It's wonderful.'

'Go on, don't make fun of me,' said Charu, forgetting one of the vital ingredients of the paan she was preparing. 'Give my notebook back.'

'Not till I've copied it and sent it to a magazine,' declared Amal.

Charu: Send it to a magazine indeed! Never.

Amal didn't relent. He kept repeating, 'It's worthy of being published,' while Charu said, in apparent hopelessness, 'I cannot argue with you. You're far too stubborn.'

'Dada must see this,' Amal averred.

At this, Charu abandoned her paan and rose to her feet swiftly; attempting to retrieve her notebook by force, she said, 'No, you mustn't read it to him. If you tell him about my writing I won't write another word ever again.'

Amal: You're wrong, bouthan. Whatever he may say, he'll be delighted to see what you've written.

Charu: Perhaps, but I don't need his delight.

Charu had vowed that she would write—and surprise Amal; she wouldn't stop until she had established the vastness of the gulf between her and Manda. Over the past few days she had written—and torn up—a great deal. Whatever she tried to write turned out to be rather similar to Amal's writing; when she compared the two, some passages appeared to have been entirely copied from Amal's pieces. Those portions were worthwhile, the rest merely an amateur's work. Assuming that Amal would laugh to himself if he read them, she had torn them to shreds and tossed them into the lake, so that not even a scrap could turn up in Amal's hands.

Her first essay had been titled 'Monsoon Clouds'. She had considered it a novel piece of writing, soaked in sensuousness.

Suddenly she returned to her senses, realizing it was nothing but a derivation of Amal's 'The Monsoon Moon'. Amal had written, 'Why doth thou skulk among the clouds like a burglar, O moon my friend?' Charu had written, 'O thou garlanded by clouds, my dearest, whence did you appear to purloin the moon and spirit her away under thy indigo garb', etcetera.

Unable to overcome Amal's influence, Charu eventually changed the subject of her essay. Abandoning the moon, the clouds, the flowers, and the birds, she composed a piece titled 'By the Temple'. There was a temple to Kali nestling in the deep shadows by the tank in the village she had grown up in; she wrote about her imaginings, her curiosity, her fears around that temple, about her many memories of it, about the legends of the powerful goddess. The beginning was full of poetic embellishments in the mould of Amal's essays, but as soon as the piece progressed her writing turned naturally simple and charged with the idioms, expressions, and nuances of village life.

Amal snatched this piece away from her and read it. He felt that the beginning was quite promising, but that the poetic tone had not been maintained till the end. Be that as it may, it was a commendable first effort.

'Let's bring out a monthly magazine, thakurpo,' proposed Charu. 'What do you think?'

Amal: How will we run it without many pieces of silver.

Charu: This magazine will cost us nothing. It won't be printed—we shall write it in our own hand. Nobody but you and I shall be published in it, nobody shall be allowed to read it; only two copies shall be produced, one for you and one for me.

Earlier, Amal would have been entranced by the prospect; but he had since lost his zeal for secrecy. He was no longer satisfied unless he wrote for the larger public. But nonetheless, he expressed his enthusiasm so as to maintain their traditional superiority. 'That will be excellent,' he said.

'But you must promise not to publish in any other magazine but ours,' Charu added.

Amal: But the editors will kill me in that case.

Charu: You think I don't have the weapons to kill you too.

It was settled, accordingly. Two writers, two editors, and two readers formed the committee.

'Let's call it *Charu's Reader*,' proposed Amal.

'No, it shall be named *Amala*.' Charu turned him down.

These plans made Charu forget her pique for some time. Manda would not be able to force herself into their monthly magazine, after all—and its doors were barred to everyone else.

Seven

Bʜᴜᴘᴀᴛɪ ᴄᴀᴍᴇ ᴜᴘ to Charu one day and said, 'Charu, we hadn't agreed to your becoming a writer.'

Startled, Charu turned red. 'I, a writer! Whoever told you that. Never.'

Bhupati: Caught red-handed. I present the evidence.

He produced a copy of *The Lake Lotus*. Charu saw that all the pieces she had collected in their private handwritten monthly magazine had been published under the author and authoress's names.

She felt as though someone had let her favourite birds out of their cage. She was enraged by Amal's treachery, forgetting her embarrassment at being caught out by Bhupati.

'And take a look at this, will you,' said Bhupati, unfolding *The Friend of the World* newspaper for her to read. It contained an article titled 'Trends in Modern Bengali Writing'.

'I'm not interested,' said Charu, pushing it away. Her indignation with Amal prevented her from paying attention to anything else. 'Try reading it,' insisted Bhupati.

Charu was forced to glance at it. The writer had penned a stern piece, roundly criticizing the oversentimental purple prose of a certain class of writer. He was particularly derisive of the style used by Amal and Manmatha Datta among them, and, comparing these with the work of the new writer Charubala Debi, had heaped fulsome praise on the natural simplicity, effortless sparkle, and skilful imagery of her language. Only emulating such a process of writing would bring salvation to Amal & Co., he had written, the alternative being inevitable failure.

'And that is what you would call outshining your mentor,' laughed Bhupati.

Although she tried to be pleased at this first ever praise of her writing, Charu felt upset instead. Her heart refused to be happy. She had to push away the delicious goblet of eulogy as soon as she had brought it to her lips.

She concluded that Amal had planned to surprise her by having her pieces published. He had decided that once a review that praised her appeared somewhere, he would show her both together to placate and encourage her. But why hadn't he displayed any interest in showing her the piece singing her praises? He had obviously been hurt by the criticism and had not mentioned the newspaper to Charu because he did not want her to read it. Charu had created a literary nook for her pleasures. The sudden storm of admiration had dropped a hailstone that threatened to shatter it. It was hateful.

After Bhupati had left, Charu sat in silence on her bed, *The Lake Lotus* and *The Friend of the World* open before her.

Amal appeared behind Charu silently, notebook in hand, to surprise her. Approaching, he saw Charu was engrossed in the critical piece in *The Friend of the World*.

Amal left again, as silently as he had come, telling himself, 'Charu is in raptures because the writer has condemned me while praising her.' His entire being seemed to turn to bile. He was infuriated, convinced that the idiot's criticism had led Charu to consider herself superior to her mentor. She should have torn that paper to shreds and burnt it to ashes.

Angry with Charu, he appeared at Manda's door, calling loudly, 'Manda-bouthan.'

Manda: Oh, come in. What a pleasant surprise. How fortunate I am.

Amal: Would you like to hear something I wrote recently?

Manda: You've kept me hoping so long to hear you read, but you never do. But maybe you shouldn't—if someone were to be angry, you're the one who'll be in trouble, not I.

'Who's going to be angry?' Amal said somewhat sharply. 'And why? Anyway never mind all that, I'm going to read now.'

Manda composed herself swiftly. Amal began to orate with much ceremony.

Amal's writing was completely impenetrable to Manda; she couldn't fathom any of it. This was why she conjured up a joyful smile on her face and listened with added enthusiasm. Encouraged, Amal's voice went from loud to louder.

He read: 'Just as Abhimanyu had mastered in his mother's womb the art of penetrating the phalanx but not that of escaping it, the river's current had learnt in the stone womb of the mountains only how to course forward, but not how to turn back. Alas the flow of the river, alas youth, alas time, alas the universe, you can only journey forward—you never retrace your steps along the path that you leave strewn with the gilded pebbles of memory. Only our consciousness looks backward into the past, the infinite universe never even spares it a glance.'

Just then, Manda observed a shadow falling on the door to her room. Pretending she had not seen it, she kept her gaze steadfast on Amal, listening to him read. The shadow vanished.

Charu had been waiting for Amal so that she could condemn *The Friend of the World* suitably as soon as he appeared, and also chide him for having broken their vow and published their pieces in a magazine.

The usual hour of his appearance passed, with no sign of him. Charu had written another piece; she wanted to read it to him; this was waiting too.

But there was his voice. Could it be coming from Manda's room? She jumped to her feet as though stricken by a bolt

33

of lightning, walking silently to Manda's door. He had not yet read to her what he was reading to Manda! 'Only our consciousness looks backward into the past, the infinite universe never even spares it a glance,' he was saying.

Charu was unable to depart as silently as she had arrived; the succession of blows had undone her completely. She wanted to shout at the top of her voice that Manda couldn't understand a syllable, that Amal's satisfaction at reading to her was nothing but stupidity. But instead of saying any of this, she announced it with loud footsteps. Returning to her bedroom, Charu slammed the door shut.

Amal paused briefly. Manda acknowledged Charu with a smile. 'Bouthan is behaving like a despot,' Amal mused to himself. 'Does she consider me her slave? Am I not allowed to read to anyone but her? This is tyranny.' With this thought, he proceeded to read to Manda in an even louder voice.

After he had finished, he passed Charu's room on his way out, observing at a glance that her door was shut. Charu realized from the sound of his footsteps that Amal had passed her room—without stopping. Her rage and indignation produced no tears. Taking her notebook, filled with her recent writing, she tore each page to shreds, piling them to one side. All this writing must have begun under an evil star.

Eight

AT DUSK, A scent of jasmine wafted in from the flowerpots in the verandah. Stars were visible through scattered clouds. Charu hadn't changed her clothes or tidied her hair. She sat in the darkness near the window, her hair blowing in the mild breeze, unable to understand the tears rolling down her face.

Bhupati entered, his face worn and his heart heavy. This was not his accustomed hour; he was usually quite late to return to his bedroom after having written his articles and corrected proofs. But that day he came to Charu as soon as evening fell, appearing to be in need of some comfort.

The lamp was unlit. In the faint light coming through the window, Bhupati could just make out Charu's figure; slowly he went and stood behind her. Charu didn't turn around despite having heard his footsteps; she remained seated, as stiff and immobile as a statue.

'Charu,' Bhupati addressed her in some surprise.

Startled by his voice, she rose to her feet quickly. She had not been expecting Bhupati. Running his fingers fondly through her hair, he asked lovingly, 'Why are you sitting alone in the dark, Charu? Where's Manda?'

None of Charu's hopes had been fulfilled all day. Convinced that Amal would come and apologize to her, she had been waiting, prepared. At this unexpected sound of Bhupati's voice, she was unable to contain herself any longer, and burst into tears.

'What is it, Charu, what is it?' asked Bhupati, alarmed.

It was hard to say. What *was* it, after all? Nothing in particular. Could she possibly complain to Bhupati that Amal had read his new piece to Manda first instead of her? Wouldn't Bhupati laugh? If there was a serious aspect to this trivial matter, discovering it was beyond Charu, who was even more distressed because she did not fully understand why she suffered so.

Bhupati: Please tell me what's wrong, Charu. Have I done something wrong? You know how disturbed I am about all the problems with the newspaper. If I have hurt you it wasn't intentional.

Charu felt restive. Bhupati was asking questions to which there was no answer. If only he would release her now.

When he didn't receive an answer even the second time, Bhupati said again lovingly, 'I cannot give you company all the time, Charu, I am guilty of that, but not any more. I will no longer devote all my time to the newspaper. You will have as much of me as you wish to.'

'That's not it,' said Charu impatiently.

'Then what is it?' said Bhupati, sitting on the bed.

Unable to contain her irritation, Charu replied, 'Never mind now, I'll tell you at night.'

After a moment's silence, Bhupati responded. 'Very well, never mind now.' He left, slowly. He had something of his own to tell her, but it remained unsaid.

Charu was not unaware that Bhupati was hurt as he left. 'Let me call him back,' she thought. But what would she tell him? She was stung by remorse, but she found no salve.

Night fell. Charu laid out Bhupati's dinner with special care, waiting for him, fan in hand.

'Braja, Braja!' she heard Manda calling loudly.

When Braja the servant answered, Manda asked, 'Has Amal-babu eaten?'

'He has,' replied Braja.

'And you haven't taken him his paan yet?' Manda began to castigate Braja.

Bhupati arrived and sat down to his meal; Charu fanned him.

She had vowed to have a cordial conversation with him, preparing the topics beforehand. But Manda's cries had distracted her from all her arrangements, and she was unable to say a single word to her husband during his meal. Bhupati, too, appeared extremely despondent and distracted, eating carelessly.

Only once did Charu speak. 'Why aren't you eating?'

'But I am,' Bhupati protested.

When they were together in their bedroom, Bhupati said, 'You were going to tell me something tonight.'

'For some time now I have been ill at ease with Manda, I daren't have her live here any more.'

Bhupati: What has she been doing?

Charu: Her behaviour with Amal is embarrassing.

'You're exaggerating,' Bhupati laughed. 'Amal is just a child, nothing more…'

'You may know what's going on in the world, but you have no idea what's going on at home. At any event, it's poor dada I worry for. Manda isn't bothered to find out whether he has had his meals or not, but if the slightest thing goes wrong with Amal's, she has a row with the servants.'

Bhupati: I must say you women are always suspecting things.

'Very well, we suspect things,' said Charu, furious, 'but I'm warning you that I shan't allow such brazen behaviour in my home.'

Bhupati was both amused and pleased at these baseless suspicions of Charu's. There was a certain refinement, a palpable dedication in this extra vigilance, this distrustful eye that the devoted wife employed to ensure that the home stayed pure, that not even the semblance of a scandal could stain conjugal existence.

Kissing Charu's forehead with affection and deference, Bhupati said, 'There'll be no need to make a fuss about all this. Umapada is going to Mymensingh to practise law, he'll take Manda with him too.'

To dispel his own worry and divert attention from this unpleasant discussion, Bhupati picked up a notebook, saying, 'Why don't you read to me what you've written, Charu?'

Snatching the notebook from his hand, Charu said, 'You won't enjoy it, you'll only make fun of me.'

Bhupati was hurt at this, but keeping his feelings hidden, he said, 'Very well, I will not make fun of you, I will be so still as I listen that you will imagine I've fallen asleep.'

But Bhupati was not heeded—and in no time the notebook soon vanished under a pile of other things.

Nine

BHUPATI COULD NOT bring himself to disclose the whole story to Charu. Umapada had been the manager of Bhupati's newspaper. Collecting subscriptions, paying dues to the printers and others and paying the servants were all his responsibility.

But one day Bhupati was astonished to receive a legal letter from the paper supplier. Apparently he owed them two thousand and seven hundred rupees. Summoning Umapada, he said, 'What's all this? I've already given all this money to you. The paper dues should not be more than four or five hundred rupees.'

'They must have made a mistake,' said Umapada.

But it could no longer be kept a secret. Umapada had been embezzling money for some time. It wasn't just the newspaper, he had run up considerable debt everywhere, claiming to represent Bhupati. He had also financed the material for a house that he was constructing in his village using Bhupati's name; most of it had had to be paid from the newspaper's funds.

Upon being caught, he said brusquely, 'I'm not running away, am I? I will pay it all back with my labour—you can name your dog after me if I leave even a penny unpaid.'

The power to desecrate Umapada's name offered no consolation to Bhupati. He was not particularly upset at having lost his money, but this unexpected act of treachery seemed to remove the ground beneath his feet.

That was the day he had visited Charu in their bedroom. He had been yearning for a moment of solace from the one person in the world he could trust. But Charu had been sitting by the window, lost in her sadness, the evening lamp unlit.

The next day Umapada made ready to go to Mymensingh. He wanted to leave quickly before his creditors learnt of his departure. Bhupati loathed him too much to be inclined to talk to him; Umapada considered his silence a boon.

'What's all this, Manda-bouthan?' Amal came to ask. 'Why are you packing furiously?'

Manda: I have to go, after all. Did you expect I'd stay here forever?

Amal: But where are you going?

Manda: Home.

Amal: Why? Something wrong here?

Manda: There's nothing wrong as far as I'm concerned. I was happy living with all of you. But others felt ill at ease.

She gestured towards Charu's bedroom.

Amal remained grimly silent.

'Oh dear, how embarrassing. What must sir be thinking?' exclaimed Manda.

Amal didn't prolong their conversation. He was certain Charu had told her husband things about him and Manda that should not have been mentioned.

Amal went out for a walk, wishing he didn't have to return to this house. If his brother had believed all that his wife had told him and considered him guilty, he would have no choice but to emulate Manda. Packing Manda off was in one sense an order of exile for him too—even if it had not been spelt out. His course was obvious to him; he should not stay another moment. But it was impossible to imagine his brother harbouring any kind of unfair impression of him. Bhupati had taken Amal into his home with implicit trust. How could

40

he now leave without assuring his brother that he had not violated that trust in any way whatsoever?

Clasping his hands to his head, Bhupati was at that moment pondering the ingratitude of members of his family, harassment by creditors, and unregulated accounts. He had no one to share this arid despair with, and was preparing to battle alone with his tormented soul as well as his debt.

Suddenly Amal stormed into his room. Bhupati was jolted out of his ruminations. 'What's the matter, Amal?' he said. He had a sudden foreboding that Amal had brought bad news.

'Has anything happened for you to doubt me, dada?' Amal asked.

'Doubt you!' Bhupati exclaimed. To himself, he said, 'The way things are, I won't be surprised if I do start doubting Amal too, some day.'

Amal: Has bouthan complained to you about my integrity?

'Is that all?' thought Bhupati. 'Thank heavens. Nothing but pique.' He had assumed another calamity had succeeded the first one. But even during a crisis, one has to pay attention to these minor issues; the world will heap obstacles in your path, but will still expect you to keep walking with your load.

At any other time, Bhupati would have made fun of Amal, but he wasn't cheerful enough today. 'Are you out of your senses?' he asked.

'Has bouthan said anything?' Amal repeated his question.

Bhupati: Even if she has said anything out of love for you, you mustn't be angry about it..

Amal: I should probably go away somewhere else and look for a job.

'You're being completely childish, Amal,' Bhupati admonished him. 'It's time for you to study now, a job can wait.'

Amal left with a glum expression; Bhupati sat down to reconcile the subscription payments with the past three years' accumulated expenses.

Ten

AMAL DECIDED HE would have to confront Charu; he would see this through to the end. He began to rehearse the severe strictures he would pronounce.

When Manda had left, Charu had determined to send for Amal on her own and appease his wrath. But he would have to be invited on the pretext of literature so she had spun out a piece in imitation of Amal's, titled 'The Light of the Dark Moon'. Charu had finally realized that Amal didn't approve of her having her own unique writing style.

Because the full moon exposed all its brightness, Charu had in her new piece rebuked it roundly, heaping humiliation on it. She had written: 'Within every layer of the immeasurable depths of the blackest night is trapped the brightness of the many-splendoured moon. Not a single beam has been lost, and hence the darkness of the new moon is more complete than the dazzle of the full moon...' etcetera. Amal revealed everything he wrote to everyone, while Charu did not—was there a hint of this in the comparison between the new and the full moons?

Meanwhile, Bhupati, the third member of this family, was visiting his close friend Motilal in the hope of deliverance from an urgent loan. Bhupati had lent Motilal a few thousand rupees during a crisis; he was extremely embarrassed to have to ask for it to be returned. Motilal was fanning himself after a bath, while performing the ritual of writing the name of the goddess a thousand times in minuscule script on a sheet of paper spread over his desk. 'How wonderful,' he said in a sincere tone when Bhupati entered, 'we hardly see you these days.'

When Bhupati told him why he was there, Motilal mulled over the matter before saying, 'What money are you talking about? Have I borrowed any money from you recently?' When Bhupati reminded him of the date of the loan, Motilal said, 'Oh, that's lapsed a long time ago.'

The world seemed to change before Bhupati's eyes. This unmasking unsettled him terribly. Just like the frightened person who seeks the highest point on land when there is a sudden flood, a doubt-stricken Bhupati beat a retreat from the outside world and entered the inner chambers of his home. 'No matter what, Charu at least will not deceive me,' he told himself.

Charu was at the time writing with deep concentration, her notebook on her pillow and the pillow in her lap. Only when Bhupati stood beside her did she become aware of his presence, whereupon she swiftly hid the notebook beneath her legs.

When the heart is already in agony, the smallest hurt exacerbates the pain. Bhupati was cut to the quick by the unnecessary haste with which Charu had concealed her notebook. He sat down slowly on the bed by her side. This unexpected obstacle to the flow of her writing and the alacrity with which she had had to hide her notebook from Bhupati prevented her from saying anything.

Bhupati had nothing to say or offer of his own today. Bankrupt, he had approached Charu empty handed like a beggar. A concerned, loving enquiry from Charu, a show of tenderness, was all he needed to salve his aching wound. But 'bounty deserted the bountiful'. When asked to unlock the store of compassion when she was least expecting it, Charu was unable to find the key. The oppressive silence between

43

them deepened the stillness of the room. After some time, Bhupati rose with a sigh and left the room without a word.

At that moment, Amal was striding swiftly towards Charu's room, having prepared several admonitions. Meeting Bhupati halfway and seeing him looking pale and stricken, Amal stopped in alarm to ask, 'Are you feeling ill, dada?'

Amal's soft, concerned query made Bhupati's heart, brimming with tears, swell in his breast. He could not utter a word. Restraining himself with great effort, he said emotionally, 'Nothing's wrong, Amal. Are you publishing anything soon?'

Amal forgot the harsh accusations he had prepared. Hurrying to Charu's room, he asked her, 'What's wrong with dada, bouthan?'

'I couldn't make out anything,' answered Charu. 'Maybe some other newspaper has criticized his.'

Amal shook his head.

Charu was comforted by Amal's unbidden appearance and the resumption of normal conversation between them. Now she broached the subject of literature, saying, 'I was writing a piece titled "The Light of the Dark Moon"; he nearly saw it.'

Charu had assumed Amal would pester her to read her new piece. She gestured with her notebook to encourage him. But Amal only gave her a sharp glance; no one knew what he was thinking, what he had surmised. He got to his feet in an instant. It was as though the traveller on a mountain trail had suddenly discovered, when the mist parted, that he was about to step into a thousand-foot-deep ravine. Without a word, Amal left the room.

Charu made little sense of Amal's unusual behaviour.

Eleven

THE NEXT DAY, Bhupati appeared in the bedroom again at an unusual hour and sent for Charu. 'We have rather a good proposal for Amal, Charu,' he told her.

Charu was distracted. 'A good...what?' she asked.

Bhupati: A proposal. For marriage.

Charu: Why, what's wrong with me?

Bhupati guffawed. 'I haven't asked Amal yet what's wrong with you. And even if he does think nothing is, I do have a minor claim, which I don't intend to relinquish easily.'

Charu: What nonsense. Didn't you say you'd received a proposal?

She turned red.

Bhupati: Would I have rushed in to inform you in that case? I would not exactly have been rewarded, after all.

Charu: A proposal for Amal? That's good news. Why put it off then?

Bhupati: A lawyer from Burdwan named Raghunath-babu wants Amal to marry his daughter and will pay for him to go to England.

'England?' Charu said in astonishment.

Bhupati: Yes, England.

Charu: Amal will go to England? That's wonderful. Excellent, very good. Why don't you talk to him about it?

Bhupati: Wouldn't it be better if you explained it to him before I talked to him?

Charu: I've told him thousands of times. He doesn't care for my advice. I cannot tell him any more.

Bhupati: Do you think he will refuse?

Charu: I've tried so many times, he hasn't agreed yet.

Bhupati: But it will not be right for him to turn this proposal down. I am in considerable debt, I cannot provide for Amal any more as I used to.

Bhupati sent for Amal. When he arrived, Bhupati told him, 'Raghunath-babu, a lawyer from Burdwan, has proposed marriage between you and his daughter. He would like to finance your visit to England after the wedding. What do you think?'

'If I have your permission,' answered Amal, 'I have no objection.'

Both Bhupati and Charu were surprised at Amal's response. Neither of them had imagined he would agree so readily.

'He is willing if his elder brother permits it,' mocked Charu. 'How obedient the younger brother is. And where was your reverence for your brother all these days, thakurpo?'

Without answering, Amal tried to smile. His silence doubled Charu's acerbity. Trying to provoke him, she said, 'Why don't you admit to your new eagerness? Why did you have to pretend all these days that you didn't want to get married? You've just been putting on an act.'

'It was out of consideration for you that Amal concealed his desire all this time, lest you feel jealous at the thought of a sister-in-law,' joked Bhupati.

Blushing, Charu protested loudly. 'Jealousy! Indeed! I'm never jealous. It's extremely unfair of you to talk like that.'

Bhupati: Look at you! I cannot even speak in jest with my own wife!

Charu: No. I despise such jests.

Bhupati: Very well, my crime is heinous. Forgive me. At any event, is the proposal to be considered as accepted?

'Yes,' confirmed Amal.

Charu: You cannot even wait to find out whether you like the girl or not. You never gave us an inkling of your desperation.

Bhupati: If you would like to take a look at the girl I shall arrange it, Amal. I've been told she is beautiful.

Amal: No, I see no need for a look.

Charu: Don't pay any attention to him. How can we have a marriage without even setting eyes on the bride? We will take a look at her, if he doesn't want to.

Amal: No, dada, I see no point in delaying needlessly over this.

Charu: No need, then a delay might break his heart. You'd better put on your wedding finery and leave at once. What if your princess were to be stolen away by another?

None of Charu's barbs could shake Amal in the least.

Charu: Is your heart longing to run away to England? Do you feel tormented here with us? Terrified? Young men today feel incomplete unless they can become Englishmen in hats and coats. Will you still recognize dark-skinned people like us when you're back from England, thakurpo?

'Why go to England otherwise?' said Amal.

'After all, we sail the seven seas in order to shed our dark skin,' laughed Bhupati. 'But don't worry, Charu, with the rest of us still here, the dark-skinned shall not lack for admirers.'

Pleased, Bhupati dispatched a letter to Burdwan at once. The wedding was finalized.

Twelve

MEANWHILE, THE NEWSPAPER had to be wound up; Bhupati could no longer finance it. In a single moment, he was compelled to abandon his pursuit of the vast, ruthless object called the people's republic, to which he had devoted himself all this time, day and night. The familiar path along which every effort of Bhupati's life had travelled without pause for twelve years, seemed to have been submerged suddenly. Bhupati had not been remotely prepared for this. Where would he now direct all his thwarted efforts? All those bygone years seemed to gaze at him like starving, orphaned children; Bhupati marched them off to the benevolent and compassionate woman he lived with.

Meanwhile, what was on the woman's mind? 'How strange,' she was telling herself, 'it's good news that Amal is to get married. But didn't he feel the slightest hesitation at the thought of leaving us after all these years, to get married and go off to England? We took such good care of him all this time, but the moment he found the slightest opportunity to escape, he took it at once, as though he'd only been waiting. And yet, such honeyed words, such a show of affection. You cannot see people for who they are. Who would have imagined that a person who can write all he did has such an empty heart?'

Comparing Amal's empty heart with the overflowing nature of her own, Charu tried to be contemptuous of him but failed. Impaled by pain, she felt all her affront, hurt, and anger rise to the surface. 'Amal will leave very soon, but still there's been no sign of him. He has not even had the time to settle our differences.' Charu kept expecting him to come back on his own—surely all their games could not end so abruptly?—but Amal never came.

Finally, when his departure was imminent, Charu sent for Amal herself.

'I'll be along in a while,' he told the maid. Charu went to the verandah and sat on the bench. Thick clouds had gathered in the sky since morning, making the day sultry. Piling her hair loosely on her head, Charu fanned herself in exhaustion.

The hours went by. Her fan could move no more. Anger, sadness and impatience swelled in her breast. 'So what if Amal doesn't come,' she told herself. But still her attention raced towards the door, every time she heard footsteps.

The church clock in the distance rang eleven. Bhupati would arrive soon for his lunch, after his bath. She still had half an hour to spare, in case Amal came. Somehow or other, their silent war had to be resolved today—Amal could not be sent off this way.

There was an eternal relationship between a brother-in-law and a sister-in-law of the same age made up of friendship, quarrels, demands, happy conversations. Was he really going to go so far away for so long a time, sweeping away the tendrils of this sheltering canopy? Would he not regret it even a little? Would he not water the soil under that canopy one last time—with the tears of their parting?

The half an hour had nearly passed. Undoing her lightly knotted hair, Charu twisted and untwisted its strands nervously around her fingers. Her tears could no longer be contained. The servant arrived to ask her, 'Will you get a fresh coconut out for babu, mathakarun?'*

---

*Traditional address for the lady of the house.

Unknotting the end of her sari where the pantry keys were tied, Charu flung them on the floor with a loud clatter. Taken aback, the servant left with the keys.

Something seemed to well up within Charu, trying to force its way up her throat.

A smiling Bhupati arrived for his lunch at the appointed hour. When she went to the spot where his meals were served, fan in hand, Charu found Amal with Bhupati. She didn't look at him.

'You sent for me, bouthan?' asked Amal.

'No, I don't need you any more,' Charu answered.

Amal: Then I'd better go, I have plenty of packing to do.

'Go,' said Charu with her eyes blazing.

With a glance at her, Amal left.

Bhupati usually spent a little time with Charu after his lunch. But as he was very busy with his accounting problems, he told her regretfully that he couldn't linger today. 'I can't stay—there's been some trouble.'

'Go, then,' said Charu.

Bhupati thought Charu looked upset. 'I don't have to leave immediately,' he said, 'but after a little rest.' When he sat down, however, he saw Charu was depressed. A penitent Bhupati stayed by her side for some time, but he was unable to start a conversation. After several failed attempts, Bhupati said, 'Amal is leaving tomorrow, you might feel lonely for a while.'

Without replying, Charu left quickly for the other room to fetch something. Waiting for a bit, Bhupati left as well.

Charu had noticed that Amal had become much thinner; the exuberance of youth had left his face completely. This gave Charu both satisfaction and pain. She had no doubt that their imminent parting was what was making him miserable; but why was Amal behaving this way? Why was he keeping himself at a distance to avoid her? Why was he deliberately making the moment of departure so discordant, so bitter?

Pondering about all this as she lay in bed, Charu suddenly sat up with a start. She had suddenly thought of Manda. What if Amal were in love with her! Was it because Manda had left that Amal was… how horrible! Could Amal behave this way? So low? So unchaste? Could he really be attracted to a married woman? Impossible! She tried to dispel the suspicion with all her might, but it gnawed at her.

Thus the hour of departure arrived. The clouds did not lift. His voice trembling, Amal said to Charu, 'It's time for me to go, bouthan. You must look after dada now. He's in a grave crisis—he has no one but you to turn to for comfort.'

Amal had learnt of Bhupati's predicament when he looked into the reason for his despondency. He was sobered when he realized how Bhupati was battling his wretched state of affairs all by himself, without anyone's support. When he thought of Charu and of himself, he turned red to the tips of his ears. Forcefully he had told himself, 'To hell with the monsoon moon and the light of the dark night. Only if I can be a barrister and return to help dada will I prove myself a man.'

Charu had lain awake all of the previous night, rehearsing what she would tell Amal when he left; she had sharpened and brightened her little speech endlessly, giving it a coating of amused indignation and cheerful indifference. But when the time came, Charu could say nothing. All she said was, 'You'll write, won't you, Amal?'

Amal touched the floor at her feet with his forehead as a mark of respect, Charu ran to her bedroom and locked the door.

Thirteen

BHUPATI WENT TO Burdwan to see Amal off to England after his wedding.

Assaulted relentlessly from all quarters, the normally trusting man had developed a certain detachment from the outside world. He enjoyed neither conferences and meetings nor the company of people. 'I have been deluding myself with all this,' he mused. 'I have wasted the time that I could have used to be happy, and consigned the essence of my life to the dustbin.'

'Just as well the newspaper is gone,' he told himself. 'I am free.' Just like the bird returning to its nest in the evening at the first sign of darkness, Bhupati abandoned his habitat of many years to return to Charu in his home. 'This is where I shall settle,' he decided, 'nowhere else. The paper ship I used to play with all day has sunk, it's time to go home now.'

Bhupati probably held the widespread belief that one does not have to assert one's right over one's wife; like the pole star, one's wife uses her own light to keep shining, without being snuffed out by the wind, not caring for fuel. When his world began to fall apart, it did not even occur to Bhupati to check for cracks in the pillars holding up his own home.

He returned from Burdwan in the evening. After a quick wash, he ate an early dinner and proceeded to smoke his hookah. Certain that Charu was eagerly anticipating the details of Amal's wedding and his preparations for the voyage to England, he waited for her; she was not here yet, probably busy with her household tasks. The tobacco fumes made the tired Bhupati sleepy. Shaking himself awake from slumber every now and then, he wondered where Charu was. Unable to wait any longer, he sent for her. 'Why so late today, Charu?' he asked her.

'Yes, I'm late today,' she replied without explanation.

Bhupati waited for Charu to ply him with eager questions; but Charu asked nothing. He was a little disappointed. Didn't Charu love Amal, then? She had been so lively when he was here, how could she have lost all interest as soon as he had left? Such contrary behaviour left Bhupati with a sudden doubt; was there no depth to Charu's feelings after all, he wondered? Did she know only to enjoy herself but not to love? It wasn't good for a woman to be so detached.

Bhupati had been happy at the friendship between Amal and Charu. The childish way in which they quarrelled and made up, their games and their conspiracies, were all sweet diversions for him. He had been pleased at the evidence of Charu's tender empathy that her constant care and concern for Amal displayed. That night he wondered in amazement whether it had all been fleeting, whether any of it had ever had any foundation in her heart. If Charu were indeed so heartless, he mused, who would offer him the shelter he himself needed so desperately?

'How have you been, Charu?' Bhupati probed gently. 'You're not unwell, are you?'

'I'm fine,' Charu answered briefly.

Bhupati: Amal's wedding is done with.

He paused. Charu tried desperately to offer a suitable response but she could think of nothing; she remained stiffly silent.

Bhupati was not normally so sensitive, but because the sorrow of parting was fresh in his mind, Charu's indifference hurt him. He had wanted to talk about Amal with Charu, who should have been suffering as well, to ease the burden on his heart.

Bhupati: She's quite pretty… Are you asleep, Charu?'

'No,' answered Charu.

Bhupati: Poor Amal had to leave all by himself. When I saw him off on the train, he was sobbing like a child—and despite my ripe age I could not contain my tears. There were a couple of Englishmen on the train, they found the sight of sobbing men extremely amusing.'

In the darkness of the bedroom, with the light put out, Charu turned on her side at first, then left the bed hurriedly. Startled, Bhupati asked, 'Are you unwell, Charu?'

Receiving no answer, he rose from his bed too. Hearing the sound of muffled sobs from the verandah, he approached swiftly to discover Charu lying collapsed on the floor, trying to hold back her tears.

Bhupati was astonished at this tumultuous outpouring of grief. 'Did I misjudge Charu?' he thought. 'She is so much of an introvert that she will not reveal her heartache even to me.' People of this nature loved deeply and suffered deeply too. Charu's love was not as demonstrative as was the case with ordinary women, surmised Bhupati. He had never seen any exhibition of emotion from her; that day he realized that it was because Charu's love flowered in secret, deep within. Bhupati was not skilled at expressing himself either; discovering the deeply private nature of Charu's emotions gave him a sense of satisfaction.

Sitting down by her side, Bhupati caressed her lightly, without a word. He did not know how to comfort her—and he did not realize that when someone tries to strangle their grief in the dark, they'd rather not have a witness to the act.

Fourteen

WHEN BHUPATI HAD retired from his newspaper, he had painted a certain picture of his future in his head. He had vowed not to do anything too ambitious; he would involve himself with Charu, with reading, with caring for her, with everyday household duties. He had planned to live quietly and peacefully, lighting up his life with little flames of happiness, with things that were accessible yet beautiful, tangible yet pure. Conversation, laughter, wit, entertainment…these things did not require much effort, but offered many joys.

In practice, such ordinary happiness is not easy to come by. Whatever cannot be purchased for a price is impossible to find unless it is already close at hand.

Bhupati simply could not become intimate with Charu. He blamed himself. 'Twelve years of nothing but journalism have made me lose my ability to be a companion to my wife,' he concluded. As soon as the evening lamps were lit, Bhupati went to his room eagerly—he said something, Charu said something, and then Bhupati did not know how to continue the conversation. This ineptitude made him feel ashamed before his wife. He had imagined that talking to her would be so simple, but to a fool like him it was so very difficult. It was easier to deliver a speech at a meeting.

It was difficult to pass the evenings that Bhupati had thought he would make romantic with laughter and entertainment, wooing and caresses. After a tortuous silence, he would actually consider leaving the room—but he couldn't, for what would Charu think?

'Would you like to play cards, Charu?' he would say.

'All right,' Charu would say, seeing no other option; fetching the cards reluctantly, she would make elementary mistakes to lose easily. There was no pleasure in such a game.

After much thought, Bhupati asked Charu one day, 'Should we send for Manda, Charu? You're rather lonely.'

Charu flared up on hearing Manda's name. 'No, I don't need her,' she said.

Bhupati smiled. He was pleased. A devoted wife never succeeded in containing her annoyance whenever she witnessed an exception in another.

Overcoming her initial loathing, Charu wondered whether she would be able to divert Bhupati better if Manda were here. The realization that she could not provide Bhupati the happiness that he sought troubled her. Bhupati had abandoned everything in the whole wide world to pin all his hopes on her. This—along with his intense effort and her own inadequacy—pained her greatly.

How could they continue this way and for how long? Why couldn't Bhupati take up something else? Why didn't he start another newspaper? Charu had not had to master the art of pleasing Bhupati; he had never demanded anything of her, never sought any particular pleasure, never made her completely indispensable to himself; now that he had suddenly placed every requirement of his life at Charu's doorstep, she seemed unable to find ways to meet them. She did not quite know what Bhupati wanted, what exactly would satisfy him; even if she had, it would not have been within her grasp.

Had Bhupati proceeded slowly, perhaps it would not have proved as difficult for Charu; but he seemed to have become destitute overnight reaching out with an empty begging bowl. This unsettled her thoroughly.

'All right, send for Manda,' said Charu. 'If she's here you will be better looked after.'

'My being better looked after!' exclaimed Bhupati. 'There's no need whatsoever.'

Disappointed, Bhupati told himself, 'I'm far too dull, I'm simply unable to make Charu happy.'

With this thought, he immersed himself in literature. When his friends visited, they were astonished to see him surrounded by Tennyson, Byron, and Bankim. They began to ridicule this sudden passion for poetry. 'The bamboo plant flowers too,' smiled Bhupati, 'even if no one can predict when.'

One evening, lighting a bright lamp in the bedroom, Bhupati hemmed and hawed in embarrassment at first, then said, 'Shall I read to you?'

'Do,' said Charu.

Bhupati: What would you like to hear?

Charu: Whatever you like.

Bhupati was a little deflated by Charu's lack of interest. Still he took courage in his hands to say, 'Shall I translate something from Tennyson for you?'

'All right,' said Charu.

It didn't work. Bhupati read hesitantly, faltering; he was unable to find the corresponding Bengali words. Charu's blank gaze made it obvious she wasn't paying attention. The small lamplit room, the evening with its promise of intimacy, did not find fulfilment.

After repeating the same mistake a few more times, Bhupati finally abandoned his literary endeavours with his wife.

Fifteen

Just as a severe blow numbs the senses, making it impossible to feel the pain at first, so too did Charu seem unable to feel Amal's absence properly in the early days of their separation.

As the days passed, however, the void left by Amal's absence grew. Charu lost her equilibrium at this terrible discovery. What desert was this that she had been transported to from her forest glade? As the days went by, the desert seemed to become even more vast.

Her heart sank the moment she awoke in the morning— she was reminded that Amal was no longer there. When she sat down in the verandah to prepare the paan, she was constantly reminded that Amal wouldn't come up behind her. Her mind wandered, she prepared too much paan sometimes, then remembered with a start that there was no one to offer them to. Whenever she stepped into the pantry, it was to recall that she didn't have to send breakfast to Amal. She would stand impatiently at the doorway to her chambers, as she used to, only to be reminded that Amal wouldn't be returning from college. There was no new book, no article, no news, no source of amusement to await expectantly. There was no one to embroider for, to write for, to buy something elegant for.

Charu was surprised at the unbearable unhappiness and restlessness she felt. Her constant despair made her afraid. 'Why, why does it hurt so much?' she kept asking herself. 'Who is Amal to me—why must I suffer on his account?

What has happened to me, after all these years; what is this that has happened to me? Even the maids and servants and labourers and porters can go back home content, why did this happen to me? Why have you put me in such a predicament, my lord?'

She continued to be surprised by the depth of her misery, which seemed neverending. Amal's memory so dominated her body and soul that there was no escaping it.

Bhupati should have protected her from the assault of Amal's memory; instead, the well-meaning fool, himself pained by the separation, reminded her of him even more.

Eventually Charu gave up completely, desisting from battling herself, acknowledging defeat; she accepted her condition and lovingly enshrined Amal's memory in her heart. Gradually, it came to pass that meditating on Amal with all her attention, with all her being, became a source of pride for her—as though the memory of her love were the greatest glory of her life.

She fixed a certain time of day for this between her various household tasks. Shutting her lonely bedroom door, she would relive every event of her life with Amal. Burying her face in her pillow, she would say over and over, 'Amal, Amal, Amal!'

A response seemed to emerge from across the seas. 'What is it, bouthan, what is it?'

Closing her tearful eyes, Charu would say, 'Why did you get angry and go away, Amal? I did nothing wrong. If you had said a proper goodbye, perhaps I would not have suffered so much.'

Speaking as she would have had Amal been sitting before her, Charu would say, 'Not for a day have I forgotten you, Amal. Not for a day, not for a moment. You have brought out the best in me, I will worship you every single day with the essence of my life.'

Thus in a chamber deep under the surface of her everyday life, in silent darkness, Charu constructed a memorial to her hidden sorrow, adorning it with garlands of tears. Neither her husband nor anyone else had the right to enter here. This spot was as secret as it was deep-rooted as it was beloved. It was here and here alone that she shed all her worldly disguises and entered as herself, unveiled and uncovered, re-emerging afterwards in the theatre of the world's laughter and conversations and activities with her mask firmly affixed to her face.

Sixteen

No longer battling with herself, Charu found a certain peace despite her immense grief and devoted herself instead to looking after her husband. While Bhupati slept, Charu would softly lower her forehead to his feet, symbolically smearing the dust of his feet on her brow. In her attention to him and to the household, she did not leave his slightest wish unfulfilled. Aware that Bhupati would be unhappy at any neglect of guests and dependants, she did not permit the smallest blemish in her hospitality. After her chores, Charu ended her day by eating leftovers off Bhupati's plate.

This attention and care appeared to revive the prematurely ageing Bhupati. For the first time, he felt like a newly-wed. Blossoming amidst all the pleasures and the laughter and the humour, Bhupati consigned his anxieties to a corner of his mind. Just as the appetite gains strength after the comforts of convalescence, the senses developing palpably, so too were exquisite and powerful sensations generated within him. Bhupati began to read poetry, keeping it secret from his friends, even from Charu. 'With the newspaper gone and after much unhappiness, I have been able to discover my wife after all these days.'

'Why have you given up writing completely, Charu?' Bhupati asked her.

'I'm not much of a writer,' Charu said.

Bhupati: Honestly, I don't see any of today's authors writing as well as you do in the Bengali language. I wholly agree with what *The Friend of the World* said.

Charu: Enough, stop.

'See for yourself,' said Bhupati, pulling out a copy of *The Lake Lotus* to compare the use of language by Charu and by Amal. Turning red, Charu snatched the paper out of Bhupati's hands and hid it in her sari.

'One cannot write without a companion,' Bhupati thought to himself. 'Wait, I have to practise writing myself, then I'll be able to rekindle Charu's interest in writing.'

Bhupati began to practise in complete secrecy. His days of unemployment passed consulting the dictionary, revising repeatedly and copying his writing over and over again. He had to put so much effort, so much suffering, into his essays that he came to believe in and love them.

Eventually, Bhupati got someone else to copy his pieces out and handed the notebook to his wife.

'One of my friends has started writing recently,' he told her. 'I don't understand all this, will you read it to see if you like it?'

Leaving the notebook with his wife, Bhupati left in trepidation. Charu saw through naïve Bhupati's deception easily.

She read them, laughing at the style and subjects. Charu had made so many arrangements to display her reverence for her husband, why did he have to squander her offerings with such childishness? Why did he have to make such efforts to earn her approval? If only he would not bother, if only he would not constantly strive to draw her attention, Charu would have found it easier to worship her husband. She earnestly wished Bhupati wouldn't debase himself, taking himself to a level lower than her.

Shutting the notebook, Charu leant back against her pillow, staring into the distance for a long time, ruminating. Amal used to give her his new pieces to read, too.

In the evening, an eager Bhupati busied himself surveying the flowerpots in the verandah outside the bedroom, without daring to ask the question.

'Is this the first time that your friend is writing?' Charu asked, on her own.

'Yes,' answered Bhupati.

Charu: They're so good—they don't seem to be first efforts at all.

Very pleased, Bhupati began to wonder how to claim the anonymous pieces as his own. His notebook began to fill up at an astounding pace. Disclosing their authorship didn't take him long, either.

Seventeen

CHARU ALWAYS REMEMBERED when letters from England were due to arrive. The first letter came from Aden, addressed to Bhupati; in it, Amal had offered respectful greetings to Charu. A letter for Bhupati came from the Suez too, Charu received respectful greetings in it as well. A letter arrived from Malta, also containing respectful greetings for Charu in the postscript.

Charu did not receive a single letter from Amal. Taking the letters from Bhupati, she read them over and over, but found not a trace of a reference to herself besides the respectful greetings.

The shelter of quiet grief, like a canopy of moonlight, that Charu had found for herself these past few weeks was shattered by Amal's callous disregard. Her heart seemed to be torn apart all over again; the stability of household duties once again gave way to disruptive tremors.

Waking up in the middle of the night, Bhupati often discovered Charu missing from their bed. Looking for her, he found her sitting by the window in the room that looked out to the south. When she saw him, she explained quickly, 'It's very warm in the bedroom, I came to catch the breeze.'

A concerned Bhupati arranged for a fan to be installed over the bed, and, fearing that Charu would fall ill, kept watch over the state of her health.

'I'm fine,' Charu would smile, 'why do you concern yourself needlessly?' She had to apply all her strength to make a smile appear on her face.

Amal arrived in England. Charu had concluded that perhaps he had not had the opportunity to write to her separately during his passage, but that he would write her a long letter once he reached England. However, the long letter did not arrive.

Every day that the post was due, Charu was restless under the routine of all her tasks and conversations. She didn't dare ask Bhupati anything, lest he say, 'There's nothing for you.'

On one of the days when the post was usually delivered, Bhupati strolled up to Charu and said with a faint smile, 'I have something, do you want to see it?'

'Show me, quickly,' said Charu, anxiously.

In jest, Bhupati refused to show her.

Impatient, Charu attempted to snatch the object from under Bhupati's shawl. 'My heart's been telling me since morning that the letter will arrive today,' Charu told herself. 'I can't possibly have been wrong.'

Bhupati's wish to tease her mounted, he circled the bed to avoid Charu's lunges.

Annoyed, Charu sat down on the bed, raising eyes brimming with tears.

Inordinately pleased at Charu's eagerness, Bhupati extracted his notebook of essays and dropped it quickly in Charu's lap, saying, 'Don't be angry, here you are.'

Eighteen

THE WORLD BECAME a bed of thorns for Charu when two postal deliveries went by without anything from Amal—although he had informed Bhupati that he would be unable to write letters for some time because of the pressure of studies.

As they spoke that evening, Charu suggested to her husband somewhat casually, 'Look, how about telegraphing England to enquire after Amal?'

'He wrote just a fortnight ago, he's busy with his studies now,' responded Bhupati.

Charu: Oh, no need in that case. I only thought, he's abroad—what if he were to fall ill or something, you never can tell.

Bhupati: No, we'd have heard if he were seriously ill. Sending a telegram isn't cheap either.

Charu: Is that so? I thought it would take a rupee or two only.

Bhupati: You have no idea, it costs about a hundred rupees.

Charu: Then there's no question.

A day or two later, Charu told Bhupati, 'My sister lives in Chinsurah these days, could you pay a visit to enquire after her?'

Bhupati: Why? Is she ill?

Charu: No, she isn't ill. But you know how much they like having you.

At Charu's request, Bhupati took the coach to Howrah Station. A row of bullock carts barred their way; at this moment, a peon whom he knew spotted him and handed him a telegram.

Bhupati was extremely alarmed to see it had come from England. Amal must be ill, he thought. Opening it apprehensively, he saw that it said, 'I am well.'

What did this mean? Examining it, he saw the reply was prepaid.

Calling off his journey, Bhupati turned his coach around and returned home, handing the telegram to his wife. Charu's face turned ashen at the sight of the telegram in Bhupati's hand.

'I cannot understand any of it,' said Bhupati. His enquiries helped him understand; Charu had pawned her jewellery to send the telegram.

'She didn't have to go so far,' Bhupati brooded. 'If she had merely requested, I would have sent the telegram, she wouldn't have had to get the servant to pawn her jewellery in the market—I don't approve of this.'

Over the next few days, Bhupati began to ask himself why Charu had become so desperate. A vague suspicion began to prick at him. Bhupati did not want to confront this suspicion directly; he tried to forget it, but the pain did not dissipate.

Nineteen

AMAL WAS WELL but still he didn't write! How had such a complete separation become possible? Charu felt the urge to get an answer directly from him, but there was an ocean between them—impossible to cross. It was a cruel separation, a hopeless separation, a separation beyond all questions, all repair.

She could keep herself afloat no longer. Tasks were left unattended, she made mistakes, the servants pilfered; observing her breakdown, people gossiped. She remained oblivious to it all.

Things came to a stage where Charu would start in surprise for no obvious reason; abandon conversations midway to go away and cry. Her face lost colour whenever Amal was mentioned.

Eventually Bhupati noticed everything as well, and finally realized what he had not considered for even a moment—his world became arid, parched, desolate.

Recalling the happy interim that had blinded him, Bhupati felt ashamed. Was this how you cheated the monkey, with pebbles because he could not tell them apart from precious jewels?

All that Charu had said and done to deceive him now came back to whip him with the words 'fool, fool, fool.'

When he finally remembered the pieces he had written with so much effort and care, Bhupati could have died of embarrassment. Like a horse being goaded, he raced up to Charu, asking, 'Where are those pieces I wrote?'

'They're with me,' answered Charu.

'I want them,' said Bhupati.

'Do you need them this moment?' asked Charu, who was frying egg fritters for him.

'Yes, this very moment.'

Taking the pan off the stove, Charu brought him all the notebooks and other papers from her cupboard.

Snatching them from her impatiently, Bhupati threw them all into the stove.

Desperately trying to extricate them, Charu said, 'What have you done!'

'Don't touch them,' Bhupati roared, clamping his hand over hers.

Charu stood by in wonder; each and every piece was burnt to cinders.

Charu understood. She sighed. Leaving the fritters unfinished, she left, slowly.

Bhupati had not planned to destroy the notebooks. But with the fire in front of him, he suddenly became violent. Unable to control himself, he had cast all the efforts of the foolishly deceived writer into the flames, under the eyes of the deceiver herself.

After Bhupati's rage had abated, and the notebooks burnt to ashes, the image of Charu's leaving the room in silence, her head bowed with grief and guilt, remained etched in his mind. Looking up, he realized Charu had been personally preparing one of his favourite meals.

Bhupati leant on the railing of the verandah. What could be more tragic in this entire world, he mused, than Charu's indefatigable attempts to please him, to maintain this deception at any cost? It was not a contemptible act on her part; to perpetrate it, the poor condemned woman had been forced to squeeze the blood out of her heart every moment, doubling and redoubling the pain of her wounded soul.

'Poor helpless girl, poor sad girl,' Bhupati reflected. 'There was no need, I didn't need any of this. All this time I did not have your love either, but I did not know it—I was happy reading my proofs and managing my newspaper, you didn't have to do all this for me.'

Withdrawing his own existence from Charu's, Bhupati began to observe her with detachment, the way a doctor treats a patient with a terrible disease. How severely this weakened woman's heart was being assailed from every direction. There was no one she could confide in, nothing that she could express in words, no one to pour her heart out to in mourning—and yet she had to bear this inexpressible, inevitable, irresistible grief, growing by the day, and go about her daily household tasks like every other person, like her unafflicted neighbours.

Entering their bedroom, Bhupati found Charu holding the window rods and staring, dry-eyed and unblinking, into the distance. Walking slowly up to her, Bhupati uttered not a word; he simply placed his hand on her head.

Twenty

'WHAT IS IT?' his friends asked Bhupati. 'You seem very busy?'

'The newspaper...' Bhupati replied.

Friend: Another newspaper? Do you want to wrap your estate in a newspaper and cast it into the river?

Bhupati: Oh no, I'm not bringing out another newspaper of my own.

Friend: Well, then?

Bhupati: A new newspaper is being published in Mysore. They have appointed me editor.

Friend: So you plan to go off to faraway Mysore? Are you taking Charu?

Bhupati: No, my uncles will stay here to look after her.

Friend: You simply cannot give up your passion for journalism, can you?

Bhupati: Everyone needs some passion or the other.

'When will you be back?' Charu asked, when it was time for him to leave.

'Write to me if you feel lonely,' answered Bhupati, 'I will come back.'

Just as Bhupati reached the door, Charu ran up to him to take his hand. 'Take me along with you, don't leave me behind all by myself.'

Halting in his tracks, Bhupati glanced at her. Her grip slackening, Charu's hand dropped from his. Bhupati retreated from her into the verandah.

He realized that, like a frightened beast pursued by a forest fire, Charu wanted to flee from the house around which the memory of her separation from Amal was still burning. 'But does she not consider my situation? Where will I flee? Am I not to be given the chance to forget in that distant land a wife who dreams of another man? Must I be by her side every single day in that place where I have no friends? When I return home after a hard day's work, how unbearable will those evenings turn in the company of a silent, grieving woman? How long can I hold to my heart someone who is dead inside? How many more days, how many more years, shall I have to live in this way? Am I not permitted to discard the ruined bricks of the home that has been destroyed, am I condemned to carry them with me forever?'

'No, I cannot do that,' Bhupati said, returning to Charu.

The colour drained out of Charu's face, leaving it like a bleached sheet of paper. She clutched at the bedpost.

Bhupati said immediately, 'Come along, Charu, come with me.'

'Never mind,' said Charu.

Dui Bon (1933)

The Two Sisters

There are two kinds of women...

Sharmila

THERE ARE TWO kinds of women, or so I've heard some pundits say.

One is mostly maternal. The other is the lover.

If you liken them to the seasons, the mother is the monsoon. She lets her gifts flow freely from the sky; bestows water, nurtures crops, quells the heat, dispels aridity, fulfils all wanting.

The lover is spring. Her mysteries run deep, her magic is bewitching. Her vivacity makes the blood tingle, entering the very core of one's being and bringing the expectant body to life, like the melody that awakens the silent veena.

Shashanka's wife Sharmila was of the maternal cast.

Her eyes were large, deep, limpid; they cast languid glances. She was like a moisture-laden cloud—ripe, delicate and verdant; the parting in her hair glowed vermilion like the morning sun; the black border of her sari was generous; on her hands she wore thick bangles inlaid with ram-head motifs. Her appearance spoke not of good looks but of good deeds.

There wasn't a single region in her husband's realm of existence—no matter how remote—over which her reign was not firm. Shielded by the wife's overprotectiveness, the husband's instincts had been blunted, making him careless. If his fountain pen slipped out of sight on his desk for even a moment, it was his wife's responsibility to recover the pen and rectify this minor disaster. Preparing for a bath, if Shashanka suddenly forgot where he had put his watch, his wife was certain to divine it. When he was about to leave the house, unwittingly having donned mismatched socks, his wife appeared at once to correct his mistake. Once, he invited friends home on the wrong day, confusing the Bengali calendar with the Western one; the responsibility of tending to unexpected guests fell on his wife. In fact, making mistakes was second nature for Shashanka, probably because he knew that any blunder he might make was bound to be corrected by her.

'I can't stand it any more,' his wife would scold him fondly. 'Will you never learn?' If he had, Sharmila's life would have certainly become barren.

Take the instance when Shashanka was visiting a friend, one evening. The clock struck eleven, then twelve—the game of bridge was in full swing. Then, suddenly his friends sniggered. 'The watchman has arrived with your summons, my friend. Your time is up.'

It was the familiar figure of Mahesh, the servant, with his grey moustache and black hair. Dressed in a loose shirt, he had a colourful dusting rag slung over his shoulder and a sturdy stick under his arm.

'Mathakurun sent me to find out whether babu is here. She's scared there might be an accident on the way back home, in this darkness. She's sent a lantern too.'

Shashanka got to his feet, throwing his cards down in annoyance. 'Poor helpless fellow,' his friends commiserated. Upon his return home, his conversation with his wife was neither pleasant in tone nor moderate in language. Sharmila accepted the rebuke in silence. What could she do, she couldn't help fretting. She simply couldn't rid herself of the apprehension that all kinds of imaginary dangers were lurking to take advantage of her absence and conspiring against her husband.

Sometimes there were visitors at home, possibly to discuss business. Tiny chits would make their appearance, at frequent intervals, from the inner chambers of the household, saying for example 'Have you forgotten you were ill yesterday? Please have your lunch quickly.'

Shashanka grew angry but also gave in to her attentions wearily. 'I beg of you, find a divinity or two to be devoted to like Mrs Chakraborty across the road,' he told his wife once, sadly. 'Your attention is too much for me alone. It would be easier to share it with the gods. They won't object, no matter how dedicated you are to their cause, but humans are weak, you see.'

'What! Don't you remember what happened to you when I went to Haridwar with Kaka-babu?' she replied.

Shashanka had described to his wife with much embellishment, how grievous his condition had been during this time. He had known that Sharmila would be as happy as she would be contrite at his exaggerated account. So how could he protest against her eloquent arguments today? He had to accept it without demur. Moreover, that very morning he had apparently displayed symptoms of a cold—or so Sharmila had imagined, forcing him to swallow ten grains of quinine and tea infused with extracts of holy basil. He had no grounds for refusing these remedies, because he had in the past raised objections in a similar situation, refusing the quinine and had subsequently run up a fever. These details in Shashanka's life history were written in indelible letters.

Sharmila was as vigorously engaged in upholding her husband's honour in the outside world as she was tenderly protective of him at home. An example comes to mind.

The couple was on their way to Nainital for a holiday. Their compartment had been reserved in advance for the entire journey. However, having changed trains at a junction and then having departed in search of a meal, they returned to discover two uniformed villains preparing to dispossess them of their compartment. At this juncture, the stationmaster arrived to inform them that the compartment actually belonged to a world-famous general; their names had been put there by mistake, he claimed. His eyes widening in panic, Shashanka was about to leave deferentially to look for an alternative when Sharmila rose to block the door, saying, 'I dare you to get me off this train. Fetch your general.'

Still a government employee at the time, Shashanka was used to maintaining as wide and safe a distance as possible from his superiors. But the more he said anxiously, 'Oh, but why bother, there are plenty of other trains, after all,' the less Sharmila heeded him. Eventually having finished his meal in the refreshment room, the general approached with a cigar in his mouth—and then retreated as soon as he saw the form of the belligerent female who challenged him from a distance.

'Have you any idea how important he is?' Shashanka asked his wife anxiously.

'I have no interest in finding out,' she retorted. 'In a compartment that belongs to us, he isn't any more important than you are.'

'What if he had insulted us?' Shashanka fretted.

'What are you here for?' his wife responded.

Shashanka was an engineer with a degree from the prestigious engineering college at Shibpur. However careless he might have been at home, he was thoroughly competent at work. The chief reason for this was that the ascendant star under whose unrelenting gaze he operated there was the person known in daily parlance as the boss. His wife was not his guiding star there and he flourished without her help. Shashanka was the acting district engineer when the unexpected arrival of a young Englishman thwarted his rise. The newcomer's relationship with—and a recommendation from—the highest authority, helped him secure the position that should have been Shashanka's, despite his lack of experience and almost non-existent moustache.

Shashanka realized that he would have to let this idiot occupy the higher position while he did the real work from the lower rungs. The superior authority slapped him on the back, saying, 'Very sorry, Majumdar, I'll find you a suitable position as soon as I can.' They belonged to the same Freemason Lodge.

But despite the assurances and the consolation, Majumdar became bitter about the whole affair. At home he was irritable about the smallest of things. All of a sudden, he began to notice cobwebs in a corner of his office; all of a sudden, he couldn't stand the particular green of the bedspread. He shouted at the servant who was sweeping the verandah for raising a cloud of dust: the cloud of dust would have appeared every day but this rebuke was new.

Shashanka didn't inform his wife of his humiliation. If she discovered it, he reasoned, she would further entangle him in the web of workplace politics—she might even have a rancorous quarrel with the authorities. She already nursed a grudge against Donaldson in particular. While trying to quell an outbreak of monkey attacks in the garden of the circuit house, Donaldson had shot a hole in Shashanka's sola hat. Although Shashanka escaped without harm, Sharmila felt he could easily have been hurt. Furthermore, people said the incident was Shashanka's fault, which fuelled her ire. Perhaps the biggest cause for her anger, however, was this—when the bullet which had been intended for the marauding monkey hit Shashanka instead, his detractors equated the two targets, deriving much amusement from it.

Sharmila found out herself about her husband being passed over for promotion. His behaviour had already led her to suspect that something was bothering him and it didn't take her long to find the root of his disquiet. 'Enough, you must resign immediately,' she urged her husband, choosing self-determination over constitutional agitation.

If only he could have resigned so easily, the stigma of humiliation would have been erased. But confronting his idealism was the guarantee of a meal from a monthly income—and the golden glow of a steady pension on the western horizon.

The year Shashanka had established himself, sailing through his MSc degree, Rajaram, his father-in-law, decided not to delay the wedding any longer. Shashanka and Sharmila were duly married. The young man then acquired his engineering degree with the assistance of his rich father-in-law. When he observed Shashanka's rapid promotions, Rajaram-babu was pleased that he had correctly predicted his son-in-law's future affluence.

In any case, it was not like his daughter had been made to feel her circumstances had changed. Not only did the couple want for nothing, Sharmila had actually maintained the lifestyle she had enjoyed while living with her father. This was because all arrangements in this domestic diarchy were under her control. She had not had a child, had probably given up hope of having one. Every month, her husband's entire income was handed over to her in one lump sum. Shashanka had no choice but to hold out his begging bowl before the goddess of wealth management at home when he needed money. Unreasonable demands were rejected outright, a verdict he had to accept without demur. The disappointment would be compensated for by tenderness in other ways.

'Resigning is easy enough. But it's you I think of, it'll put you into great difficulties ,' said Shashanka.

'It'll make me even more upset to swallow the pain of humiliation,' Sharmila responded.

'But I have to work, if I give up a secure job where will I find another one?'

'I'm sure it exists, it's just that you're not aware of it. You think the universe doesn't extend beyond the deserts of Baluchistan, which you so drolly call Lichistan.'

'Heavens! That universe is enormous! Who dares survey its roads? Where will I get a pair of binoculars powerful enough?'

'You don't need powerful binoculars. My distant cousin Mathur-dada is a contractor in Calcutta; a partnership with him will take care of our needs.'

'It will be an unequal alliance. The weights are far lighter this side of the scales. Forcing a partnership will only mean a loss of face.'

'There'll be nothing whatsoever lacking on this side. You know very well that the money my father left me has grown in my bank account. You can certainly match your partner.'

'How can I do that? It's your money, after all,' exclaimed Shashanka rising. There were people waiting for him.

Tugging at his clothes to make him sit down again, Sharmila said, 'But I'm yours too.'

'Pull out your fountain pen from your pocket,' she continued. 'Here's a notepad, write your resignation letter. I won't rest till you put it in the post.'

'You won't let me rest either, it appears.'

He wrote out his resignation letter.

Sharmila left for Calcutta the very next day, arriving at Mathur-dada's house. 'You never bother to ask after me,' she accused him. 'You don't either,' a woman would have said to compete. That response didn't occur to a man. He accepted his offence. 'I don't have even a minute to spare,' he said. 'I forget my own existence sometimes. Besides, you people live so far away.'

'I read in the papers that you've got a project to build a bridge in Mayurganj or is it Mayurbhanj,' continued Sharmila. 'It made me so happy. I wanted to congratulate you in person.'

'Not just yet, little girl. It's premature.'

This was the situation—the project needed investment. Initially drawn up in partnership with a rich Marwari trader, it turned out to be an agreement which gave the partner the meat and Mathur the bones. Hence the attempt now to withdraw.

'This cannot be allowed,' said Sharmila in concern. 'If you must have a partnership, do it with us. It'll be very unfortunate if such a good project were to slip through your fingers. I will never let it happen, no matter what.' Mathur's heart melted and the formalities didn't take much time after this.

The business proceeded apace. Shashanka had shouldered the responsibility of employment before, but that responsibility was limited. He had had a master then, the demands made of him were matched by what was due to him. Now he was in his own employment, demands and dues merged. His days no longer alternated between work and leisure; time was now a single entity. The hold that responsibility had over him was all the stronger precisely because he could give it up whenever he wanted to. He simply wanted to repay his debt to his wife, after which he could slow down. Wearing his watch on his left wrist, a sola hat on his head, rolled up sleeves, khaki trousers, a belt at his waist, thick-soled shoes, dark glasses—Shashanka devoted himself body and soul to his work. Even when he was on the verge of repaying his wife, he continued to forge ahead.

Earnings and expenditure used to flow in the same channel earlier but now two streams were formed—one flowing bankward and the other, homeward. The monthly allocation for Sharmila remained unchanged; the mysteries of debit and credit were beyond Shashanka in this department.

Now business and the leather-bound ledger that recorded its dealings were a remote fortress for Sharmila. No harm in that. But with the orbit of her husband's work life outside her circle of domesticity, her rules and regulations began to be disregarded. 'Don't work too hard,' she pleaded, 'you'll collapse.' This had no impact. Surprisingly, he wasn't collapsing either. Sharmila fretted over his health, bemoaned his lack of rest, became obsessed with the minutiae of his comforts. Completely ignoring these wifely concerns, Shashanka drove off swiftly early each day, in his second-hand Ford, tooting his horn. He came back home to scoldings at two or two-thirty in the afternoon, swallowing his lunch just as quickly.

One day his car collided with someone else's. He was safe but the car was dented, and he dispatched it for repairs. Sharmila was frantic. 'You mustn't drive any more,' she told him tearfully.

'Having someone else at the wheel will not necessarily make it any safer,' Shashanka replied, laughing it off.

Another day, while he was supervising a renovation job, a nail from a broken packing box pierced the sole of his shoe and lodged itself in his foot, and he went to the hospital to be bandaged and take an anti-tetanus injection. Sharmila burst into tears. 'Stay in bed just a day,' she urged him.

'Work,' said Shashanka tersely; he couldn't have been more brief.

'But…' said Sharmila. He left without another word, his foot still bandaged.

She didn't dare insist on anything any more. The man of the house had begun to assert himself in his own domain. Looming above all her arguments and entreaties was that one statement—'I have work to do.' Sharmila lived in a state of needless anxiety. Whenever he was late, she feared another accident. When her husband was sunburnt, she assumed it was influenza. Tentatively, she hinted at seeing a doctor—stopping herself when she saw her husband's expression. These days she didn't even dare vent her concern to her heart's content.

Shashanka began to look lean and dry, as though he had been stripped down to his bones. His attire became shorter and tighter, so did his spare hours; his speech was as brief as sparks of fire. Sharmila tried to keep up with this faster rhythm. She had to keep food warm by the stove all the time, for her husband could say at any odd hour, 'I'm off now, I'll be late.'

Soda water and tins of dry food were always kept in the car. A bottle of eau de cologne was placed prominently within view, in case of a headache. But an examination of the car upon Shashanka's return revealed that none of it was ever used. Clean, folded clothes were displayed in the bedroom every morning quite prominently, but despite this, on at least four days a week he had no time to change into fresh clothes. Household discussions had to be compressed like Morse code, that too while trailing behind him as he moved about the house, desperately urging him to pay attention before he left.

Whatever tenuous ties Sharmila had had with the business were now severed; her money had been returned with interest. The interest had been calculated down to the last paisa and a receipt obtained for the payment. 'Dear god!' exclaimed Sharmila to herself. 'Men cannot give all of themselves even in love. Their pride has to hold then back.'

Shashanka used some of his recently acquired profits to construct a house after his heart in Bhawanipur: his latest fancy. He was constantly thinking up schemes for the home—all to surprise Sharmila. She didn't fail to be suitably surprised either. The engineer installed a machine to wash clothes, and Sharmila admired it effusively after examining it but told herself, 'The clothes will go to the washerman just as they do now. I can cope with a donkey, I cannot cope with science.' The potato-peeling instrument amazed her too. 'Seventy-five per cent of the pain of cooking potatoes is now gone,' she had remarked. The instrument was found later, consigned to retirement along with the pans and dented kettles.

When the house was completed, Sharmila's love—suppressed all this while—found release in this inanimate object; bricks and wood were eternally patient. Two servants wore themselves out arranging the furniture and decorating the house; one of them actually left. The rooms were done up solely with Shashanka in mind. He hardly spent time in the drawing room any more but cushions in different styles were laid out for his tired back; there were countless flower vases, and the tables and stools were covered in tasselled fabric with floral prints. Shashanka no longer appeared in the bedroom during the day for in his new almanac Sunday was nothing but Monday's twin; when there was no work to be pursued anywhere else on certain holidays, he managed to discover things that could be done at home, sitting down in his office with the oil paper used for drawing plans or with his ledgers.

Older traditions were maintained, nevertheless: a pair of silk slippers lay in attendance in front of the thickly cushioned sofa. The paan was still arranged in its container as before, the clothes-stand had a fine silk kurta and crisp dhoti draped over it. It required some courage to intervene in the office but Sharmila ventured in, duster in hand, while Shashanka was away. Her efforts at bringing about an equilibrium between decoration and discipline amongst the phalanx of useful and redundant objects in the office continued, unabated.

Sharmila still looked after Shashanka, though largely invisibly. Her self-sacrifice, so palpable once, now showed itself indirectly: in decorating the house, in maintaining the garden, in the silk coverlet on the cot Shashanka sat on, in the floral pattern on his pillowcase, in the blue crystal flower vase on the corner of the desk in his office which held marigolds.

With great unhappiness, she had to present her offerings at a distance from her shrine. Only recently she had been badly hurt, shedding secret tears afterwards. It was the fourteenth of November—Shashanka's birthday and the most important occasion in Sharmila's life. Their friends were invited as usual, their home was decorated specially with flowers.

Back home for lunch after his morning's work, Shashanka remarked, 'What's going on? Is there a dolls' wedding tonight?'

'Oh god, have you forgotten it's your birthday?' replied Sharmila. 'I won't hear a word, you shall not go out this evening.'

'Business bows before no day besides the one on which you die,' was the response.

'I'll never ask you again,' she pleaded. 'But I've invited people for this evening.'

'Look, Sharmila, don't try to turn me into a toy that you can play with before a room full of people,' said Shashanka. He left, taking large, rapid strides. Sharmila locked herself in her bedroom and cried for hours.

When the guests arrived in the evening, they accepted the greater demand of business quite easily. If it had been Kalidasa's* birthday, they would certainly have considered his compulsion to write the third act of *Shakuntala* nothing but a bad excuse. But this was business! There was plenty of entertainment anyway. Nalu-babu mimicked stage actors and made everyone laugh uproariously; even Sharmila joined in the laughter. Shashanka's Shashanka-less birthday prostrated itself reverentially before a Shashanka-managed business.

Despite her unhappiness, Sharmila, too, surrendered to the flag flying on Shashanka's work chariot, which raced away at a distance. For him work was a pursuit of that unattainable goal that cared for nothing—not the wife's pleas, not the friend's invitation, not even one's own comfort. For a man, respect for work is a form of self-respect, a way to devote himself to his skills. From the line that divided her domestic world from his, Sharmila observed with awe Shashanka's labour on the other

---

*Famous Sanskrit poet and dramatist. *Shakuntala* is his best known work.

side. He had taken himself far beyond the boundaries of his home, extending his work to distant lands, employing hundreds of people. Man battles with his fate every day; if a woman's tender arms attempt to hold him back from that perilous trail, he has no choice but to break out of the embrace ruthlessly.

Sharmila accepted this ruthlessness respectfully. Sometimes she couldn't control herself—her love and anxiety made her intrude where she had no right to. Inevitably she was rebuffed which she accepted as her due, and returned dejected. She prayed to the gods to 'watch over him' in all the places where she was not permitted.

Nirad

Just as the affluence of the family was racing towards six figures, riding on its bank deposits, Sharmila was afflicted by an obscure disease, robbed of the strength to even stay on her feet.

The reason for everyone's anxiety over this illness must be elaborated. Sharmila's father, Rajaram-babu, was a zamindar* whose land spanned several tracts in the district of Barishal and near the delta of the river Ganges. He also held shares in a shipbuilding enterprise at the Shalimar docks. He had been born at the confluence of the old and new eras. Once an expert at wrestling, hunting, and fencing, he was well known for his mastery of the pakhwaz**, and could recite from memory entire pages from *The Merchant of Venice*, *Julius Caesar*, and *Hamlet*. He idolized Macaulay's English and he was mesmerized by Burke's oratory, though his reverence for the Bengali tongue didn't run beyond the epic verse, *The Slaying of Meghnad*†. In middle age he had considered alcohol and forbidden meats an intrinsic aspect of the modern diversions of life, but in old age he gave them all up. His clothes were always immaculate, his countenance pleasing and serene, his body tall and muscular, his temperament social. He could never bring himself to turn down a request of any kind. He had no faith in religious

*Feudal landlord.
**Indian, two-headed drum.

†*Meghnadbadh Kavya* (1861)—The famous epic-verse by Michael Madhusudan Datta.

rituals, although they were conducted with much pomp and ceremony in his home. The ostentation was enough to signal his lineage; the rituals were for the womenfolk and others. He could easily have got himself the title of 'raja', and when asked the reason for his indifference to the idea of nobility, Rajaram would say with a smile that he was already enjoying the title bestowed on him by his father; giving precedence to any other title would be an insult to this one. In any case, his welcome at Government House was always accorded at a gatehouse reserved for special guests. Important British administrators ate and drank champagne in copious quantities, during the Jagatdhatri puja at his residence.

After Sharmila's wedding, his widower's home was occupied by his son Hemanta and his younger daughter Urmimala. The son's looks made heads turn and he was described by his professors as brilliant. There wasn't a subject in which he had not attained the highest level of success in his examinations. Moreover, there were strong signs that he would uphold his father's reputation when it came to physical prowess. Needless to say, a constellation of young girls orbited expectantly around him, but his heart was indifferent to marriage; his latest aim was to collect degrees at a European university. It was with this objective that he began to study French and German.

With no other academic degree left to read for, he had started on law—though completely unnecessarily—when something in his stomach or one of his organs began to give trouble. Doctors could make no headway. The stealthy disease seemed to have found a fortress-like home in the young man's body, and it proved as difficult to locate as to attack.

Rajaram had unshakeable faith in a particular English doctor of the time who had built a reputation for surgery. The renowned doctor began to investigate his patient's body. Accustomed to wielding the scalpel, he immediately

89

concluded that the danger was deep-rooted and that surgery was needed. But the region that was skilfully uncovered by the scalpel revealed neither a foe nor any signs of malicious activity. It was too late to rectify the error—the young man died.

His father's grief would not be quelled. The death did not completely destroy him, but he was utterly devastated by the memory of his son's treatment. The image of such a vital, beautiful, strong body being carved up in this fashion wrapped its talons around his mind like a ferocious, black bird of prey. Sucking out his life force, it forced him towards death.

A freshly minted doctor—and Hemanta's former classmate—named Nirad Mukherjee had assisted in looking after the patient. Insisting all along that the prescribed treatment wasn't correct, he had made his own diagnosis, advising a long sojourn in dry climate. But Rajaram's superstitions had remained unshakeable. He had believed that the only suitable adversary of death in a difficult battle could be an English doctor. So this incident made his affection and respect for Nirad climb, disproportionately, to new heights. His younger daughter Urmi, too, suddenly felt this man's genius was extraordinary. 'See, baba, how much confidence he has in his own abilities even at this age,' she told her father. 'What pure courage he has displayed in opposing the formidable English doctor's viewpoint!'

'Medical science isn't learnt from textbooks alone,' agreed her father. 'Some people have a rare, god-given gift for it. Nirad is one of them.'

Their reverence for him began thus, with some slight proof, with the potency of the blow dealt by grief, with the pain of penitence. Then it swelled on its own, without waiting for supporting evidence.

One day, Rajaram said to his daughter, 'Urmi, I can hear Hemanta calling out to me all the time, "Let people not suffer from disease." I've decided to establish a hospital in his memory.'

'Wonderful idea,' said Urmi, bursting with her usual enthusiasm. 'Send me to Europe to learn medicine and take charge of the hospital when I return.'

Rajaram was touched. 'The hospital will be dedicated to the gods, and you will be its priestess. Hemanta suffered so much before dying, he loved you so much, this pious mission will bring peace to his soul in the other world. You looked after him day and night when he was ill, the care you took of him then will be manifold under your supervision.'

That a girl from an orthodox family should become a doctor didn't seem unusual to the stricken old man. He had fathomed, deep in his heart, what it meant to be able to save people from illness. His son may not have survived, but if other people's sons did, it would be some compensation; it might lighten his suffering a little. 'I'll send you to Europe as soon as you've completed your science courses at the university here,' he told his daughter.

One particular thought, with regard to the remarkable young Nirad, occupied Rajaram. He was a real gem. The more he saw of him, the more he liked him. He may have got his degree, but he had left all that far behind to plunge himself into the ocean of medical sciences. He was young but entertainment and other diversions couldn't entice him. He would discuss every recent development, test it out himself, and do untold damage to his medical practice by neglecting patients. He was supremely contemptuous of those who managed to grow their practices. 'Idiots earn success,' he said, 'but the deserving earn glory.' He had discovered the aphorism in a book.

Eventually Rajaram said to Urmi one day, 'I've thought it over, I think if your work at the hospital is done as Nirad's wife the effort will be complete, and I will be relieved too. Where will we find another one like him?'

Whatever else he might do, Rajaram could not turn his back on Hemanta's viewpoint. Hemanta used to say that when

91

it came to marriage, ignoring the daughter's choice to impose the parents' preference was barbaric. Earlier Rajaram had argued that marriage was not just a personal matter, the entire family was involved, therefore it was necessary to be guided not just by choice but by experience. No matter what he had said then, no matter where his preference had lain, his love for Hemanta was so strong that it was the son's wish that won.

Nirad Mukherjee had been a regular visitor to their family home for a while. Hemanta had given him the nickname of Owl. When asked for an explanation, he'd say, 'The man is mythological, he's ageless, he's all knowledge, that's why I refer to him as Minerva's mount.'

Nirad had been present at tea at their house on occasion, had engaged in furious debate with Hemanta, and must have acknowledged Urmi at the back of his mind but not in his behaviour, because the traditional response in such cases was not in his nature. He could discuss things but he couldn't converse. If he possessed the warmth of youth, he lacked its dazzle. This was why he took pleasure in contemptuously ignoring those vigorous young men whose youth shone forth. For these reasons, no one had had the courage to consider him a member of the club of suitors for Urmi. Yet it was this perceptible indifference—added to the present reason—that had extended Urmi's respect for him to the frontiers of reverence.

So when Rajaram announced that he would be happy if his daughter were to be married to Nirad, provided she had no objection, Urmi had nodded to indicate she was favourably disposed to the idea. All she added was that the wedding should be the culmination of her studies in India and then abroad. Her father said, 'That's an excellent notion, but I'd be relieved if the engagement were to be finalized through mutual agreement before that.'

Nirad's consent didn't take long to secure, although his behaviour implied that betrothal was an enormous sacrifice for the scientist, almost tantamount to suicide. Possibly as a means for mitigating this crisis somewhat, it was agreed that Nirad would direct Urmi on academics as well as everything else—that is to say, gradually cast her in the mould of his future wife. And that too scientifically, under rigorous discipline, like the infallible processes followed in a laboratory.

'Birds and beasts have emerged from the factory of nature as finished products,' Nirad told Urmi. 'But human beings are raw material only. Man himself has the responsibility to build something with it.'

'All right, test me,' said Urmi deferentially. 'You will encounter no resistance.'

'You have different kinds of abilities,' said Nirad. 'They have to be channelled and guided around the prime objective of your existence. Only then will there be meaning to your life. You will succeed in reining in distractions with the power engendered by motivation, while displaying integrity and dynamism—only then can that unity be termed a moral organism.'

A delighted Urmi compared him to the numerous young men who had been visitors at tea, or to their tennis courts, but never said anything worth thinking about; at best they could yawn when someone else did. In truth, Nirad was pretentious. But no matter what others might think, Urmi considered everything he said significant and profound.

Rajaram frequently asked his elder son-in-law to join them in their gatherings at home, attempting to get the two men acquainted. 'That young man is insufferably presumptuous; he considers all of us his students—and that too languishing in the far corner of the last bench,' Shashanka told Sharmila.

'You're just jealous.' Sharmila smiled. 'Why, I quite like him.'

'Why don't you change places with your younger sister?' Shashanka laughed.

'Maybe you'll breathe a sigh of relief in that case, but not I.'

Nirad's brotherly love for Shashanka didn't appear to be growing either. 'He's a mechanic, he's no scientist,' he said to himself. 'All hands, no brains.'

Shashanka frequently bantered with his sister-in-law over the subject of Nirad. 'It's time to change your name,' he said.

'Under the Western system?'

'No, under the pure Sanskrit system.'

'And what's this new name?'

'Bidyutlata. Nirad will like this electric vine. He's already familiar with electricity in his laboratory, now the vines will bind him down at home.'

To himself he said, 'The name does suit her.' He felt a pinprick somewhere. 'What a pity she's being claimed by such a prig.' It was difficult to say whose claim would have provided satisfaction and comfort to Shashanka's tastes instead.

Rajaram died soon afterwards. Niradnath, future owner of Urmi's rights, applied himself to the task of improving her mind with utmost concentration.

Urmimala looked even prettier than she actually was. The brightness of her intelligence sparkled through her restlessness. She was curious about everything. If she was interested in science, she was no less—possibly more—interested in literature. She was very keen on watching football matches but didn't ignore the cinema. When an authority on physics came to lecture at Presidency College, she was present there too. She listened to the radio regularly—she might scoff at the music, but she was curious about it. When the groom was on his way to get married, accompanied by a musical band, she would run to the balcony for a glimpse. She visited the zoo frequently; it was great entertainment, especially at the monkeys' cage. When her father had gone fishing, she had stood by him, holding the fishing rod. She played tennis, was expert at badminton. All this she had learnt from her brother.

She was like a slim tendril in motion, shaking at the slightest of breezes. She dressed simply and neatly. She knew how to arrange her sari with just the right amount of tightness, wrap it a little differently around herself, straighten it out in places, so as to look alluring while retaining her mystique. While she couldn't sing very well, she played the sitar. No one could tell whether the music was for listening or watching; her animated fingers seemed to make the strings speak in unison. She never lacked for things to talk about, never needed a reason to laugh. She had an extraordinary talent for giving company to people, single-handedly compensating for anything that was missing. Only in Nirad's presence, now, did she become a different person; the wind in her sails died down, she could only move gently, slowly, guided by the oars.

Everyone said Urmi was as lively as her brother. She knew it was Hemanta who had taught her to think freely. He used to say that Indian homes were nothing but moulds to produce clay puppets—no wonder that the English could make three hundred and thirty three million of them dance to their strings. 'When my turn comes,' he would proclaim, 'I shall destroy this society of puppets like a heretic.' His turn never came but his spirit had stayed alive in Urmi

This led to trouble. Nirad's ways of doing things were extremely rigid. He arranged a rigorous academic schedule for her. 'Look, Urmi, don't let your concentration spill as you travel along this road,' he edified her. 'Or else the pitcher will have nothing left by the time you reach your destination.' 'You flit around like a butterfly,' he accused her. 'You gather nothing. There's no need to be a bee. You have to make every moment count; life isn't a pleasure cruise, after all.'

Nirad had recently procured books on pedagogy from the Imperial Library, books that contained philosophical edicts such as these. The language he used was the language of books, for he had no natural expression of his own.

Urmi was left in no doubt of her guilt. Hers was a noble mission and yet how easily she was distracted! She castigated herself repeatedly. Nirad was a living example before her—what astounding determination, what focus on his goals, what stern rejection of any manner of entertainment or pleasure. If he spotted a storybook or some light literature on her desk, he confiscated it immediately. On a visit to supervise Urmi, he was told she had gone for a matineé performance of Sullivan's opera, *Mikado**. When her brother was alive, she had leapt at such opportunities. Nirad had taken her to task suitably that day, telling her grimly in English, 'Look, you have taken the responsibility of dedicating your life to making your brother's death worthwhile. Have you forgotten already?'

Urmi felt extremely remorseful. 'What extraordinary insight this man has,' she mused. 'I no longer grieve intensely—I didn't realize it myself. Shame on me! Am I so frivolous?' To ensure restraint, she decided to banish all embellishment from her clothes. The saris turned coarse, all traces of colour disappeared from them. She gave up the chocolate she craved, though she had so much of it stacked in her drawer. Firmly confining her recalcitrant will to a narrow orbit, she tethered it to the arid stake of responsibility. Her sister rebuked her; while the choice epithets that Shashanka showered on Nirad were in an unrestrained foreign tongue not to be found in the dictionary, nor pleasant to the ear.

There was one similarity between Nirad and Shashanka. When Shashanka's urge to heap abuse on someone intensified, his preferred language was English; when Nirad's subject was edification, he only used pedantic English. What Nirad found most objectionable were Urmi's occasional visits to her sister's house. Not only did she visit Sharmila every now and

---

*The Mikado (1885)—Famous comic opera by W.S. Gilbert and Arthur Sullivan.

then, she did it eagerly. The familial relationship Sharmila and Shashanka had with Urmi undermined Nirad's own relationship with her.

'Look, Urmi, don't be offended by what I'm about to tell you,' Nirad told Urmi gravely, one day. 'What can I do, I have a responsibility, the call of duty forces me to say unpleasant things. I want to warn you that maintaining regular relations with Shashanka-babu is unhealthy for the development of your character. You may be blinded by the charm of the family connection, but I can clearly see disaster lying ahead.'

The document certifying that Urmi's purity had already been pawned lay in Nirad's safe. So, any tarnishing of it would have meant a loss for him alone. Because they had been forbidden, Urmi's visits to Bhawanipur became rare, conducted on different pretexts. This self-discipline on her part was like paying a debt. And as for Nirad, what could be greater self-denial for a disciple of science than the responsibility for her life that he had undertaken forever, compromising his own quest in the process?

Urmi had somehow managed to endure the agony of forsaking all attractions. Yet she felt an occasional surge of unhappiness which she could not explain away as mere restlessness. All Nirad ever did was give her instructions, why couldn't he devote himself just to her for a moment? It was for such worship that her heart yearned—its absence prevented her soul from being satiated, took the joy out of all her tasks. Sometimes Nirad looked at her with ardour, as though it wouldn't take much longer, as though the deepest mystery of life would be revealed any moment. But the Almighty knew—even if those aching depths did exist somewhere within him—that Nirad did not know its language. Since he could not express it, he was contemptuous of desire. He considered it a display of strength, a matter of pride, that he could come away without a word despite holding his heart in turmoil. 'Sentimentality is not my cup of tea,' he proclaimed. Urmi felt like crying on those occasions but such had been her training that she, too, reverently labelled this behaviour as bravery, mercilessly castigating her own failing heart. Yet no matter how hard she tried, it flashed upon her that the stern resolve she had willingly imposed on herself in an hour of grief had weakened with time, forcing her to cling to Nirad's willpower for support.

'Look, Urmi,' Nirad would tell her clearly, 'remember that you have no hope of receiving from me the compliments and flattery that ordinary women expect from men. What I shall give you is far truer, far more valuable, than these manufactured endearments.' Urmi would sit in silence, her head bowed. 'Can I keep nothing hidden from this man?' she would reflect.

Still she couldn't subdue her heart. She went up to the terrace for solitary walks. The afternoon light turned to grey. Moving beyond the peaks and troughs of the houses in the city, the sun set on the far side of the masts of the ships moored in the distant river. Daylight disappeared gradually. The moon rose above the spire of the cathedral; in the barely discernible light, the city grew dreamlike, like a ghostly palace of illusions. Was life really so rigid, so harsh, she questioned herself. And was this man really so miserly that he would allow her neither escape nor emotion? Suddenly she felt rebellious, she wanted to break the rules, to shout out aloud, 'I don't believe in all this.'

Urmimala

NIRAD'S RESEARCH PROJECT was completed. He sent his thesis to a European science society. Offering fulsome praise, they gave him a scholarship. He decided to travel abroad for a degree from a foreign university.

There were no heart-rending exchanges when he said farewell. All he would say repeatedly was, 'Now that I'm going away, I'm sure you'll slacken in your work.'

'Don't worry,' said Urmi.

'I'm leaving a detailed note on how to conduct yourself, how to study,' Nirad said.

'I will follow it to the letter,' responded Urmi.

'I want to take those books away from your cupboard and lock them up in my home.'

'Do,' said Urmi, handing him the keys. Nirad glanced briefly at the sitar too but hesitated and stopped.

Eventually he had to speak again out of his overwhelming sense of responsibility. 'I have just one concern—if you start visiting Shashanka-babu's home again there's no doubt that your dedication will be compromised. Don't imagine I'm speaking ill of Shashanka-babu. He's a very nice man. Not many Bengalis can match his head for business or his passion for it. His only fault is that he doesn't believe in principles. Really, I feel quite worried for him at times.'

This led him to enumerate many of Shashanka's faults; nor could Nirad conceal his grievous anxiety that these flaws—hidden today—would be revealed one by one, in alarming proportions, as Shashanka grew older. But in spite of that, Nirad wished to acknowledge openly that Shashanka was a very nice man. He also wished to add that Urmi needed to protect herself properly from their dissolute company, from the atmosphere in their home; if her sensibilities were to descend to their level, it would amount to a moral downfall.

'Why do you worry so much?' asked Urmi.

'Do you want to know why? You won't be angry?'

'You have given me the strength to accept the truth. I know it isn't easy, but I must bear it.'

'Then let me tell you. I have noticed that there's a similarity in your nature and Shashanka-babu's. He is extremely good-humoured. Isn't that what you like about him?'

Is this man omniscient, wondered Urmi again. There was no doubt that she liked her brother-in-law very much. Shashanka laughed loudly, knew how to tease her, to make fun of her. And he knew exactly which flowers were Urmi's favourites, and which colours she liked her saris in.

'Yes, I do like him, that's true,' she admitted.

'Sharmila-didi's love is gracious and dignified, she tends to people as she tends to the gods, she never abandons her responsibilities. It is under her influence that Shashanka-babu has learnt to work with concentration. But the days that you visit Bhawanipur his mask slips. He gets into skirmishes with you, he removes the pin in your hair to let it loose, the moment he spots your textbook he puts it on the top shelf of the cupboard. The urge to play tennis suddenly rears its head, even if there's work to be done.'

Urmi had to admit that it was Shashanka-da's impishness that made her like him so much. The child in her seemed to come alive whenever he was near. She didn't spare him from her demanding ways either. Her sister smiled her calm, gracious smile at their boisterousness. Sometimes she scolded them mildly too, but this was just pretence.

'You'd do better to remain where your natural instincts aren't indulged,' concluded Nirad. 'If I were still here I wouldn't have worried, for my nature is diametrically opposed to yours. I would never have allowed your mind to rot for the sake of your heart.'

'I will heed your warning constantly,' said Urmi, her head bowed.

'I'm leaving a few books with you,' Nirad told her. 'Read the chapters I have marked carefully, they'll prove useful afterwards.'

Urmi was in need of this assistance. She had been assailed by pangs of doubt, telling herself, 'I may have made a mistake in my first flush of enthusiasm. Maybe a career as a doctor will not suit my disposition.'

The books, with Nirad's notes jotted in the margins, would pin her down, helping her swim against the current.

After Nirad's departure, Urmi became even harder on herself. She practically locked herself indoors, except for going to college. The more her tired brain wanted to rest after a long day in the classroom, the more strictly did she lock it up in academic chains. She made no progress with her studies, her mind roved futilely over the same page over and over again—but still she wouldn't admit defeat. Nirad's willpower exerted its influence on her even more from a distance.

She censured herself most strongly when she found herself distracted by old memories. She had had many admirers amongst the young men. She had ignored some of them at the time, felt drawn towards others. No romance had ensued, for the desire for romance had only wafted over her heart like the capricious breeze of spring. And so she had merely hummed to herself, copied poetry she liked into her notebook, played her sitar when she had felt very restless. Now at times, even while her eyes were trained on her book, she would be startled by thoughts of a man she had not deigned to even acknowledge at the time, whose constant attention had once annoyed her. Today it was his very fervour that seemed to fan her dissatisfaction, just as the short-lived wings of the butterfly give flowers a taste of spring before departing.

The harder she tried to banish these thoughts, the more an equally strong counterforce brought them back. She had placed Nirad's photograph on her desk; she would gaze at it intensely. His expression held the sparkle of intelligence but no fire of passion. If he wasn't going to call out to her, whom would her heart respond to? She kept up her silent incantation, 'What talent! What immense sacrifice! How pure of character! How incredibly fortunate I am!'

It is necessary to mention that Nirad had scored a victory himself in one particular area. When his marriage to Urmi had been arranged, Shashanka and many other sceptics had laughed mockingly. Rajaram-babu was naïve, they had observed; he had mistaken Nirad for an idealist. His grandiloquent aphorisms could not conceal the fact that his idealism was roosting in Urmi's treasure chest. Certainly he was sacrificing himself but to a god whose abode was the Imperial Bank. We inform our fathers-in-law directly that we need money, we explain that the money will not go waste but be used in the service of their daughter. But this gentleman was a saint: he claimed he would marry for a saintly cause. And then he would go on to translate that cause in his father-in-law's chequebook.

Nirad had known such comments were inevitable. 'I shall marry you on one condition,' he had told Urmi. 'I won't accept a single rupee from you, my own income shall be my only sustenance.' His future father-in-law had proposed sending him to Europe but he wouldn't agree. As a result, he had to wait a long time. 'Please give the money you wish to contribute towards establishing the hospital to your daughter. I shall not accept a salary for taking charge of the hospital. I am a doctor, I do not need to worry for a living.'

Rajaram's admiration for him had strengthened at this speech and Urmi had nearly burst with pride. Sharmila turned antagonistic towards Nirad, stoking Urmi's pride further. 'Hmmph!' she said. 'I'd like to see how long the vow is kept.' Thereafter, whenever Nirad spoke in his pompous manner, Sharmila would suddenly flounce out in the middle of the conversation, her back stiff. Her footsteps could be heard retreating into the distance. For Urmi's sake she didn't actually say anything but her silence spoke volumes.

Initially Nirad had sent five or six pages of detailed instructions by every post. Some time later, an unexpected telegram arrived. It was an urgent demand for a large sum of money for his higher education. Urmi's pride was dented, but she found some consolation too. The more the days went by and the longer Nirad's absence became, the more her real nature looked for openings through the barbed wire of her tasks. She deceived herself under various pretexts, repenting afterwards. Coming to Nirad's aid during such periods of low self-esteem offered comfort to her repentant heart.

Handing the telegram to the manager of the estate, Urmi said tentatively, 'The money, kaka-babu.'

'It's baffling,' said the manager. 'We were under the impression that this money was untouchable.'

He didn't like Nirad.

'But abroad...' Urmi couldn't finish.

'I know habits inculcated in this country can change in another—but how will we keep pace,' replied the manager.

'He might be in trouble if he doesn't get the money.'

'All right, my dear, I'm sending the money, don't worry. This may be the first time, but I can assure you it's not the last.'

That it wasn't was proved soon afterwards by a larger demand. This time it was on grounds of ill health. 'It would be better to discuss this with Shashanka-babu,' the manager said grimly.

'In no circumstances must didi or Shashanka-da learn of this,' said Urmi, in alarm.

'I'm not keen on taking this responsibility all by myself.'

'One day it will all be his, after all.'

'We must ensure it isn't all gone by then.'

'But we have to consider his health too.'

'You can be unhealthy in different ways, I cannot quite fathom which one this is. If he were to return, the change of air might do him good. Let us send him a return passage ticket.'

Urmi was so perturbed at the prospect of Nirad's return that she put it down to her unwillingness to having his noble mission interrupted midway.

'I'll send the money this time,' said the manager, 'but I suspect this will worsen the doctor's health.'

The manager was a not-too-distant relative. His hint struck a discordant note in Urmi and she felt a pang of doubt. 'I'll probably have to tell didi,' she mused. Meanwhile, she kept berating herself. 'Why am I not suitably upset?'

Sharmila's illness had become a matter of concern by this time. Her brother's fate had frightened her. Different doctors tried to unearth the abode of the disease from various perspectives. 'The criminal will slip through the hands of the CID, the innocent will die under the knife,' said Sharmila with a tired smile.

'Let them continue investigating, but the regular way—no surgery in any circumstances,' said Shashanka, with a worried expression.

Shashanka had two big projects on hand at this time. One was at a jute mill by the river. The other was near Tollygunge, at the new country house of the zamindar of Meerpur. The living quarters for the labourers at the jute mill were to have been completed within three months. Several borewells had to be sunk at different spots. Shashanka didn't have a moment to spare. But he was frequently held back by Sharmila's illness, although his anxiety about work mounted.

They had been married for such a long time but Sharmila had never been ill enough for Shashanka to have to worry. So his disquiet over this illness made him as restless as a child. Instead of going to work he would wander around before sitting down helplessly at Sharmila's bedside. Massaging her temples, he would ask, 'How do you feel?'

'Don't worry, I'm fine,' she would respond at once. The response wasn't believable, but Shashanka believed it at once and escaped, simply because he wanted very much to believe it.

'I have a big project from the king of Dhenkanal,' said he. 'I have to discuss the plan with his minister. I'll be back as soon as possible before the doctor visits.'

'Swear by me you're not going to neglect your work and rush back,' complained Sharmila. 'I know you need to go. You must or else I won't get better either. There are enough people here to look after me.'

The desire to build a business empire surged within Shashanka constantly. The attraction for him, however, was not wealth but greatness. The métier of the male is revealed only in his accomplishments and the business of earning money becomes irrelevant only when it is nothing but a way to spend the day. People at large respect wealth only when it towers over everything else; it is not the advantages that wealth brings, it is the enormity of the achievement that gives them joy.

At the very moment that he sat anxiously by Sharmila's bed, Shashanka couldn't help wondering where trouble might be brewing in his empire. Sharmila knew these concerns signalled not a mind obsessed with petty concerns, but the determination of the male ego to erect a victory column on the lowlands of personal circumstances. She gloried in Shashanka's glory too. So, though it was a matter of joy for her that her husband was neglecting his work to take care of her, she didn't enjoy it. She kept sending him back to his battlefield.

On her part, Sharmila was perpetually anxious about how well her household was being run. Who knew what the servants and cooks were up to while she languished in bed. She had no doubt that rotten ghee was being used in the kitchen, that the hot water for the bath wasn't being put in the bathroom on time, that the bedclothes hadn't been changed, that the cleaning man wasn't clearing the drains properly. She knew full well how everything went out of control if you didn't refer to the list when the washerman brought the laundry back. Unable to contain herself, she would leave her bed to investigate; the aches in her body would increase, her fever would escalate, the doctor could not fathom why.

Eventually Urmimala was summoned by her sister. 'Never mind your college for a while, come and rescue my home. Or else I cannot even die in peace.' Those who are reading this history will chuckle at this point, saying, 'I see.' It does not need much intelligence to realize that the inevitable happened, and this turn of events was all it needed. There was no reason to assume that fate would play its role without showing its hand to Sharmila.

'I'm going to look after my sister.' Urmimala felt a new zeal. She had to put aside all other tasks for the sake of this new responsibility. There was no choice. Moreover, it had occurred to her that the task of looking after her sister was an extension of her future mission of being a doctor.

With much ceremony, she took a leather-bound notebook along with her; it had lines drawn in it to record the daily ups and downs of the illness. Lest the doctor ignore her for her inexperience, she resolved to read up as much as she could about her sister's disease. Since the subject of her MA course was physiology, she would have no difficulty in following medical terms. So, confident that her mission would not be compromised in the course of taking care of her sister—that, on the contrary, she would be pursuing that very mission with greater application and concentration—she packed her books and notes and arrived at her sister's house in Bhawanipur. But she never got the opportunity to flip through the thick book on medicine in which her sister's illness should have been included. Even specialists were unable to identify her ailment.

Urmi assigned herself the role of disciplinarian. 'It's my job to ensure that the doctor's instructions are followed. You have to do as I say, I'm warning you,' she informed her sister gravely.

Sharmila smiled at her younger sister's solemn display of responsibility. 'Really? Who's this teacher who taught you to be so serious? You must be a new disciple—that explains the fervour. I've brought you here for you to do as I say. Your hospital isn't ready yet, but my household is. Take charge of it for now, give your sister a little rest.'

She forcibly evicted Urmi from her sickbed.

Urmi now held the post of representative in her sister's domestic kingdom. There was anarchy everywhere and it required swift redressal.

All members of this household, great or small, were meant to dedicate themselves in service completely to the man who reigned at its summit. Sharmila simply could not shed her conviction that the man in question was completely helpless and lamentably inefficient at looking after his physical needs. It was laughable, but she turned emotional when she saw him absent-mindedly setting his sleeve on fire with his cigar, oblivious to what he had done. The engineer left for work at dawn, leaving the tap running in the corner of the bedroom in his rush after brushing his teeth. On his return he found the floor awash with water, the carpet ruined. Sharmila had objected to the location of the tap from the very beginning. She knew this man would create a muddy mess not far from his bed. But since he was an accomplished engineer, he had boundless enthusiasm for making every problem more complex on the grounds of scientific convenience. Once, struck by a sudden brainwave, he made a stove from a completely original design of his own. It had one door this side, and one more, the other; one chimney on the left, and another to the right; an economical way for the fire to blaze on one side, a sloping passage for the burnt ashes to fall on the other side—and along with all this, niches, cavities, and techniques in various sizes and forms to bake, fry, boil, and warm. She had had to accept the stove as an expression of passion, not for use, but for maintaining peace and conviviality. Shashanka was like all adults playing at being children, throwing tantrums if prevented from getting his way, but forgetting it all in a day or two. Such men never chose the tried and the tested, always created preposterous things, and it was the responsibility of the wives to agree in words and do as they wished in deed. Sharmila had borne the responsibility of looking after such a husband with great pleasure all these years.

They had spent so many years together. Sharmila could not imagine Shashanka's world without her in it. Now she was worried that the messenger of death might force a separation between that world and its nurturer. She even feared that the inevitable neglect of Shashanka's needs after her death would prevent her disembodied soul from finding peace. Fortunately, Urmi was available. She wasn't as calmly capable as her sister. But still, she was managing on Sharmila's behalf. And the things she was doing were meant for women to do. Men were never satisfied to have their daily needs met without the tender touch of a woman; it all seemed mechanical. When Urmi peeled and sliced apples with her lovely hands, when she arranged the orange slices on one side of the white stone plate, when she broke open a pomegranate and laid out its pips with care, Sharmila seemed to see herself in her sister. From her bed, she issued a constant stream of instructions to Urmi.

108

'Please refill his cigarette case, Urmi.'

'Can't you see he hasn't even remembered to change his dirty handkerchief for a clean one?'

'See now, his shoes are stuffed with dirt and sand. Doesn't even remember to order the bearer to clean them.'

'Change the pillowcases, there's a dear.'

'Throw the paper scraps into the dustbin.'

'Check his office, will you, I'm certain he's left the key to his cashbox on his desk.'

'Don't forget the cauliflower seeds for the garden.'

'Tell the gardener to trim the rose bushes.'

'I can see a white mark on the back of his coat—wait a moment, will you, what's the hurry—Urmi, brush the coat, dear.'

Urmi was used to spending her time on books, not on household work, but she found all this very amusing. Having emerged from the rigid discipline under which she had been living, the work here appeared fun to her. She had no idea of the anxieties, the commitments, in this household; those thoughts were only on her sister's mind. This was why these tasks were like a game, a sort of holiday, full of small pleasures. This world was completely distinct from the one she had occupied. Here no finger was wagged at her; and yet the days were filled with tasks, tasks with variety. She made mistakes, forgot things, but no stern admonition awaited her. Even if her sister tried to scold her, Shashanka laughed it off, as though there was something very enjoyable about Urmi's slips. As a matter of fact, household chores were no longer considered onerous responsibilities; a casual air prevailed, mistakes didn't matter. This was a matter of great comfort and amusement to Shashanka. It felt like a picnic. Urmi didn't fret over anything, wasn't apologetic, wasn't embarrassed, was amused by everything; this lightened the ordeal and burden of Shashanka's work. As soon as his working day was over, or even if it was not, he was drawn back home.

It had to be admitted that Urmi was not entirely competent at household chores. But it could be observed that, even though they weren't her forte, she made up for something that had long been missing in this house—although it was difficult to put in words what exactly it was that had been missing. This was why Shashanka felt a wave of carefreeness in the air when he came home. This freedom was evident not just in the way the home was tended to or in moments of leisure alone, but also in its particular pleasures. Essentially, it was Urmi's playful cheerfulness that made up for all that was missing, that lent vibrancy to the days and nights. Always vivacious, she quickened the work-weary Shashanka's blood.

Urmi's awareness that Shashanka found pleasure in her company gave her joy too. This was the happiness she had been missing all this time. She had long since forgotten that she could make someone happy simply on the strength of her own existence, and along with it, had forgotten her own worth too.

Shashanka's mind was now like the river caught between the high and the low tide. His pace of work stilled. He could no longer be heard repeating anxiously that any delay or obstacle would be disastrous, leading to losses. When he did express such apprehension, Urmi dispelled his grimness with her laughter, asking, 'Did the ogre visit today, that supplier of yours in the green turban—was he here to threaten you again?'

'How did you know of him?' Shashanka would ask in surprise.

'I know him very well. After you left the other day, he was waiting in the verandah. I kept him amused with this and that. His home is in Bikaner, his wife died when her mosquito net burned down, he wants to get married again.'

'In that case I will make sure not to be home when he comes. Until he locates a bride he can keep spinning his dreams.'

'Tell me what you need from him, the way he behaves with me, I think I can persuade him to do it.'

Even if the fat figures in Shashanka's profit ledger—now above ninety and still climbing—showed signs of slowing down at times, he wasn't perturbed. Shashanka Majumdar's passion for the radio had been unknown all this time; when Urmi forced him to listen every evening, it no longer seemed frivolous and a waste of time. Early one morning he had to go all the way to Dum Dum to see planes take off and land— scientific curiosity was not the main attraction. He received his initiation into shopping at New Market. Sharmila used to buy her groceries there sometimes; she considered this kind of shopping her department. She had neither imagined, nor expected, that Shashanka would help her. But then Urmi didn't go there to buy anything specific, only to rummage among the shelves and to bargain. If Shashanka wanted to buy her something she snatched his wallet from him, putting it in her own bag.

Urmi had no regard for Shashanka's work ethic. He berated her at times for preventing him from working. The outcome was so catastrophic that Shashanka had to devote twice as much time to undoing the sulk that followed. On the one side were Urmi's tears, on the other, the unavoidable demands of work. Caught in this crisis, he tried to complete all his work in his chamber before returning home. But staying there beyond the afternoon was unbearable.

Whenever he happened to be particularly late, Urmi's rage took the form of distant withdrawal behind an unbreachable silence. Her indignation and unshed tears gave secret pleasure to Shashanka. Innocently he would exclaim, 'Urmi, you must maintain your silent revolt. But by Jove, you never vowed not to play,' appearing with tennis rackets. When close to victory, Shashanka would deliberately lose the match. The next morning, he would repent wasting his time.

One afternoon, Shashanka was bent over a difficult plan at his office desk. He was holding a red-and-blue pencil in one hand while running his fingers redundantly through his unkempt hair, when Urmi arrived to tell him, 'I've fixed it with that middleman of yours to take me to the Pareshnath temple. You come too. Please.'

'Not today, please, I simply cannot now,' Shashanka pleaded.

Urmi wasn't the least bit in awe of the importance of his work. 'So this is your chivalry—no hesitation in handing over a helpless woman defenceless into the clutches of Green Turban!'

Eventually Shashanka gave in to her insistence, abandoning his work to drive her in his car. Sharmila was very annoyed when she got to know of such intrusions. She believed that the uninvited entry of the woman into the realm of the man's work was unpardonable. Sharmila had always considered Urmi a child. She persisted with this thought even now. Maybe she *was* a child, but the office was not the place for childishness. She summoned Urmi to reprimand her in rather strong terms. Such a rebuke might have produced results, but upon hearing his wife's angry voice Shashanka himself appeared at the door, reassuring Urmi by winking at her repeatedly. Pointing to the pack of cards in his hands, he signalled to her, 'Come away to the office, I'll teach you poker.' It wasn't at all the hour for a game, nor did he really have the time or the inclination. But he seemed even more distressed than Urmi by her sister's stern words. He could have kept her at bay himself by coaxing and cajoling her, or even scolding her mildly, but it was very difficult for him to accept Sharmila's taking Urmi to task.

'How can you give in to all her demands,' Sharmila berated Shashanka. 'At all odd hours of the day or night…your work will suffer terribly.'

'Poor thing, she's a child,' said Shashanka. 'She has no companion here, how will she survive without any diversions?'

There was more to Urmi than childishness. When Shashanka sat down to his plans, she would draw up a stool, saying, 'Teach me.' She understood easily, the mathematical formulae not appearing complex to her. Very pleased, Shashanka set her problems, which she solved. When Shashanka was going to take the steam launch to inspect the progress at the jute mill, she demanded, 'I want to go too.' Not only did she go, she also argued over the calculations and measurements. Shashanka was thrilled. This was more enjoyable than having to wax lyrical. He was no longer anxious when he brought work home from his chamber. He now had a companion for his drawing and calculations. With Urmi by his side, the work progressed. Not rapidly, true, but the time devoted to it seemed worth the effort.

Sharmila was dealt a huge blow. She understood Urmi's childishness, indulged the flaws in her household management, but since she herself considered it mandatory for the wife to keep herself at a distance from the husband when it came to business, she didn't at all approve of Urmi's unrestricted access. This was nothing but arrogance. The Gita referred to staying within one's limits as morality. At the end of her tether, she asked her sister one day, 'Tell me, Urmi, do you really enjoy all those drawings and calculations and tracing?'

'I really do, didi.'

'Hah, enjoy indeed,' said Sharmila disbelievingly. 'You just pretend to like it to please him.'

Maybe so. Sharmila did approve of Shashanka's being taken care of in terms of clothes and food and attention, but this kind of pleasure didn't sit well with her notions.

'Why do you waste time with her?' she asked Shashanka repeatedly. 'Your work suffers. She's a child, how will she understand?'

'She doesn't understand any less than I do,' answered Shashanka. He thought that praise for her sister would please Sharmila. Fool!

When Shashanka had neglected his wife because of the demands of his work, Sharmila had not only accepted it as inevitable but had also felt a certain pride about it. She had largely resisted the insistence of her own heart, which yearned to envelop her husband in a cocoon of attention. Men are the royal tribe, she used to say, they must constantly expand the powers they are born with so as to achieve the impossible. Or else they will be reduced to a level inferior to women. Women fulfil their ordained place in the world quite naturally with their inherent tenderness, with the wealth of love they are born with. But men have to fulfil themselves through daily battles. In the past, kings would set out even without provocation to expand their empires. Not because they coveted larger kingdoms, but to reassert their male glory. Women had better not come in the way. Sharmila had not obstructed Shashanka's progress; she had consciously cleared the way in his journey towards fulfilling his ambition. Once she had covered him in her web of tender care; but she had since unravelled the web herself, even if unwillingly. She still took care of him lovingly but stayed invisible in the background.

But alas, what kind of capitulation was her husband displaying day by day? She couldn't see everything from her sickbed, but there were enough indications. Even a glance at Shashanka's expression showed he was completely mesmerized. How had this slip of a girl managed to dislodge this work-obsessed man from his mission so easily? Her husband's inability to command respect was more painful now to Sharmila than her illness. The original arrangements for looking after Shashanka—his food, his clothing, his comforts—had by now fallen into disuse. The kind of food that he considered particularly delicious was suddenly missing from the dinner table. Justifications were provided but they had never been entertained before. Slips like these used to be unpardonable, worthy of the sternest censure—a household that was once so disciplined had been so transformed that today, even the most serious of flaws appeared to be a farce. Whom could she blame! Just as Urmi was seated on a stool in the kitchen, supervising the cooking according to her sister's instructions—with a discussion about the cook's past also in progress—Shashanka arrived to announce, 'Never mind all this now.'

'Why, what must I do?'

'I'm free this afternoon, let's go and see the Victoria Memorial. I'll explain to you what's absurd about it.'

This strong temptation immediately attracted Urmi, ever ready to play truant. Sharmila knew that her sister's absence from the kitchen would not make the slightest difference to the quality of the meal—but a fragrant touch would have enhanced Shashanka's satisfaction. What use was it talking about satisfaction, though, when it was clear with each passing day that satisfaction had become irrelevant; that her husband was happy.

This was what made Sharmila fretful. Tossing and turning on her sickbed she told herself repeatedly, 'Now I know, as I'm about to die, that whatever else I may have achieved, I haven't succeeded in making him happy. I had expected to see myself in Urmimala, but she isn't me, she's a completely different woman.' Gazing out of the window, she mused, 'She has not taken my place, I cannot take hers. My going may hurt him, but her going will mean he'll lose everything.'

As she mused, she became conscious that winter was approaching; the warm clothes would have to be put out in the sun. She sent for Urmi, who was playing table tennis with Shashanka.

'Here's the key, Urmi,' she said. 'Go put the warm clothes out in the sun on the terrace.'

Urmi had barely put the key in the lock of the cupboard when Shashanka arrived. 'Later, there's plenty of time for all that. Finish the game first.'

'But didi…'

'All right, I'll get permission from didi.'

Didi extended her permission and a long sigh with it.

'Put a cold compress on my forehead,' she instructed the maid.

Although Urmi seemed to have forgotten herself now that she had found a release, once in a while she would abruptly be reminded of the demanding duties of her life. After all, she wasn't really free; she was, in fact, still bound to her mission. As she was to the person whose authority she had submitted to. It was he who had chalked out the details of her daily tasks; Urmi could not deny his permanent jurisdiction over her life. While Nirad had been present, this had been easy to acknowledge; she had had the strength for it. Now her determination had deserted her—but her sense of responsibility still nagged her. And the oppressive responsibility made her even more hostile to it; since it was difficult to forgive herself for her sins, she indulged in the sins further. To numb her pain, she thus distracted herself by amusing herself with Shashanka. When the time comes everything will fall into place on its own, she reasoned, but never mind all that as long as this holiday lasts. Then, once in a while, she shook her head violently, pulled her books out of her trunk and bent over them. After which it was Shashanka's turn. Snatching the books out of her hands, he put them back in the trunk and sat on it.

'Very bad, Shashanka-da,' said Urmi. 'Don't waste my time.'

'I waste time in trying to waste your time,' countered Shashanka. 'We're even.'

116

After a few attempts to retrieve her books, Urmi gave in, not averse to the idea. But despite this, she was tormented by her sense of duty for the next five or six days—then her willpower weakened again.

'Don't imagine I'm weak, Shashanka-da,' she said. 'I'm determined to keep my vow.'

'Meaning?'

'After my degree here I'm going to Europe to study medicine.'

'And after that?'

'Then I'll establish the hospital and take charge.'

'And whom will you take charge of? That fellow named Nirad, that insufferable…'

Putting her hand on his mouth, Urmi said, 'Hush. If you talk like that I'm going to quarrel with you.'

Fortifying her resolve, Urmi said to herself, 'I have to be true, I have to be true.' She considered being untrue to her relationship with Nirad, which her father himself had fostered, nothing short of philandering.

But the trouble was that she received no support from Nirad. Urmi was like a tree clinging to the earth but deprived of light, its leaves robbed of colour. She became impatient at times, wondering why the man couldn't even write her a proper letter.

Urmi had spent years at a convent school. Whatever her shortcomings, she was accomplished in English and Nirad knew as much. This was why he had resolved to overwhelm her with his use of the language. Had he written in Bengali he might have averted disaster but the poor fellow didn't know that he didn't know English. Garnering grandiloquent words, compiling unwieldy, pedantic phrases, he would transform his sentences into heavily laden bullock carts. Urmi found it funny though she was embarrassed to laugh; it was snobbish to find flaws in the English used by a Bengali, she would reproach herself.

When he was still in the country, Nirad's manner of dispensing advice had given their encounters an air of gravity. The profundity of this advice was surmised by Urmi rather than evident to her. But long letters offered no room for surmise. Puffed-up words lost their weight, the heavy noises only betraying the lack of things to say.

This behaviour of Nirad's, which she had become accustomed to when he was in the country, was what hurt her the most when it came from a distance. The man simply didn't have a sense of humour. Its absence was starkly obvious in his letters. And comparisons with Shashanka in this respect came to mind naturally.

An occasion for such a comparison had become available just the other day. While searching for her clothes, she discovered, at the bottom of her trunk, an unfinished pair of woollen slippers. Her memory went back four years. Hemanta was still alive. They had all been on holiday in Darjeeling, everyone enjoying themselves; Hemanta and Shashanka had kept up an unending stream of jokes and laughter. Urmi, who had recently learnt how to knit, was knitting a pair of slippers for her brother's birthday. Shashanka used to tease her about it constantly. 'Gift your brother anything else you want, but not slippers, please. They signify disrespect for those elder than you, said the sage.'

'Then whom would the sage rather have me disrespect?' asked Urmi, with a sidelong glance.

'The traditional claimant to disrespect is the brother-in-law,' responded Shashanka gravely. 'You are in debt to me already. The interest has been multiplying.'

'I don't remember anything like that.'

'You aren't supposed to, you were a mere adolescent then. Which is why you were unable to take on the mantle of the ringleader on the bride's side, that night on which this fortunate man was wedded to your sister. And undelivered slaps from that pair of tender hands have now materialized in the form of this pair of slippers created by that same pair of hands. I'm staking my claim to them.'

The claim was not honoured, the slippers were laid at her brother's feet. Then, some time later, Urmi received a letter from Shashanka. It made her laugh a great deal. She still had the letter in her trunk. Unfolding it, she read it again.

You left blithely yesterday, but no sooner had you left than calumny was heaped on you, which I consider my duty not to keep secret from you.

Many people have observed a pair of local slippers on my feet. But they have observed even more closely the sharp talons on my toes poking through the holes in them like the moon on a cloudless sky. (Vide Bharatchandra's *Annadamangal*. Doubts about the aptness of the metaphor will be arbitrated by your sister.) When Brindaban Nandy from my office touched my sandalled feet with his fingertips to convey his reverence, the degradation in my standing reverberated in my mind. I asked the servant, 'On which interloper's feet has my other pair of slippers assumed a life of its own?' Scratching his head, he replied, 'When you went on holiday with Urmi-mashi's family, those slippers went as well. When you returned, only one of the pair came back with you, the other one...' His face turned red. 'All right, enough,' I admonished him. This exchange took place in the presence of several people. Stealing shoes and slippers is a base act. But the human heart is weak, greed unstoppable, we often do such things, God probably forgives us. Still, if the theft reveals intelligence, the stain of misdeed is lightened. But one of a pair of slippers! Shame!!!

I have concealed the name of the perpetrator of this crime as much as possible. If the person in question were to protest loudly, displaying their usual garrulousness, word will get out. Climbing a slippery slope over slippers is worthwhile only if the heart is innocent. You can silence critics like Mahesh at once with the help of a pair of artistically crafted slippers, as befits his audacity.

I enclose my foot size.

After receiving the letter Urmi had got down to knitting the woollen slippers, with a smile, but she had never finished them. She was no longer keen. Discovering them today she decided to gift him the unfinished pair on the anniversary of their holiday in Darjeeling.

The day was just a few weeks away. A deep sigh escaped her—how distant, alas, were those days of bright laughter, when she had floated on wings of air. All that stretched before her now were relentlessly harsh and dry, duty-strewn days.

It was the seventh of March, Holi. When he was engaged in his work in small towns, Shashanka had no time for such celebrations, they would forget all about the occasion. This day, Urmi had put a touch of aabir—the traditional coloured powder—on her sister's feet as she lay on her bed. Then, on the prowl for Shashanka, she discovered him working intently in his office, hunched over his desk. Creeping up behind him, she smeared his hair with the powder, staining all his papers. A contest ensued. There was red ink in an inkpot on the desk. Shashanka emptied it on Urmi. Grasping her hand, he seized the bundle of aabir knotted to the end of her sari and daubed it on her face, and then began the chasing, the jostling, the shrieking. The hours passed, baths and lunch were forgotten, the sound of Urmi's high-spirited laughter resounded all over the house. Fearing that Shashanka would have an accident, Sharmila eventually dissuaded them through a string of messages.

The day was done. It was late at night. The full moon had risen in the cloudless sky over the tangle of gulmohar branches. All the trees in the garden rustled as they swayed in a sudden gust of wind, the web of shadows beneath joining in. Urmi sat silently by the window. Sleep eluded her. The blood had not stopped pounding in her breast. The scent of mangoes swamped her senses. Like the myrtle yearning to bloom on this spring night, Urmi too seemed to have turned into a quivering mass. She went into the bathroom to pour cold water over her head, rub herself down with a wet towel. Tossing and turning on her bed, she finally sank into a dream-filled slumber.

Urmi woke up at three in the morning. The moon was no longer visible in the window. The room was dark within, while the row of trees outside stood in light and shadow. Urmi felt tears welling up within her, refusing to cease. Burying her face in her pillow, she sobbed. These tears from her heart had no words, no meaning to be expressed through language. If asked, would she even know where these torrents of yearning had arrived from to churn her body and her heart, sweeping away the day's labour, the night's blissful slumber?

The sun was streaming into the room when Urmi awoke. Her morning chores were neglected. Sharmila forgave her on grounds of exhaustion. What remorse was it that had left Urmi fatigued today? Why did she feel defeat was approaching?

'I'm not able to do what you want me to, didi,' she told Sharmila. 'I can go back home if you like.'

Sharmila couldn't say, 'No, don't go.' Instead, she said, 'All right, you might as well. Your studies are being hampered. Come over now and then to check on things.'

Shashanka was out on work, Urmi took the opportunity to return home. Shashanka returned that day with a set of equipment for drawing machines. They were for Urmi, he was supposed to teach her this art. Not finding her in her usual place, Shashanka went to Sharmila's room to ask, 'Where's Urmi gone?'

'She cannot study here, she's gone home,' said Sharmila.

121

'But she knew that when she came here. Why did it suddenly occur to her now?'

Sharmila realized from his tone that he suspected her. Not wanting to argue in vain, she said, 'Tell her I asked her to come back. I'm sure she won't object.'

At home, Urmi found a letter from Nirad awaiting her. She didn't dare open it. She knew full well she was guilty of many sins. She had cited her sister's illness earlier as her reason for breaking the rules. For some time now the justification had all but become a lie. Shashanka had stubbornly insisted on engaging two nurses for Sharmila—one for the day and one for the night. Following the doctor's instructions, they prevented the family from streaming in and out of the patient's room constantly.

Urmi knew Nirad wouldn't consider the pretext of her sister's illness serious enough. 'That's not relevant,' he would argue. Indeed it wasn't relevant— 'I'm not really needed there.' Penitently, she resolved to herself, 'I'll accept I'm wrong and beg forgiveness. I will promise never to repeat the mistake, never to break the rules again.'

Before opening the letter she pulled out Nirad's photograph again, placing it on her desk. She knew Shashanka would mock her if he saw. But Urmi simply would not be embarrassed by his taunts; this was her atonement. In her sister's house, she had suppressed all references to her forthcoming marriage to Nirad. They didn't bring it up either—for the subject was unpalatable to them. Today, Urmi determined to broadcast the information unambiguously through all her actions. She had kept her engagement ring hidden for some time. Retrieving it, she put it on. It was rather a cheap ring, the glory of Nirad's personal poverty had made it more valuable than a diamond one. His implicit claim was, 'The ring doesn't determine my worth, it's my worth that determines it.'

Having purified herself thus as much as possible, Urmi slit the envelope open slowly.

After reading the letter, she leapt in the air. She wanted to dance, but wasn't in the habit. Her sitar lay on the bed; without tuning it, she began to play it loudly, without attention to melody.

Entering at that precise moment, Shashanka asked, 'What is it? Has the wedding day been finalized?'

'Yes, Shashanka-da, it has.'

'No chance of changing it in any circumstances?'

'None at all.'

'Then I'd better arrange for the music and the sweets right away.'

'You needn't make any arrangements.'

'You'll do it all by yourself? Hail warrior-princess. And the gift for the bride?'

'I've paid for it already.'

'The bride's organizing her wedding herself? I don't quite understand.'

'Here you are, you will now.'

She handed him the letter. Shashanka burst out laughing after reading it.

Nirad had written that the complex research to which he wanted to dedicate himself could not be conducted in India. Therefore he was being compelled to accept another enormous sacrifice in his life. There was no choice but to call off his wedding to Urmi. A European woman was willing to marry him and devote herself to supporting him. But the mission was the same, whether accomplished in India or in England. Sending him a small portion of the money that Rajaram-babu had earmarked for the mission would do no harm. On the contrary, it would be a mark of respect for the departed soul.

'If occasional largesse can keep the man alive in that distant land, that would be best,' said Shashanka. 'Or else there's the fear of his rushing back, hungry and desperate.'

'If that's what you fear, you can send the money—I'm not parting with another penny.' Urmi laughed.

'You won't change your mind again, will you?' asked Shashanka. 'The resolute princess's pride will stand tall, won't it?'

'How does it matter to you if I do change my mind, Shashanka-da?'

'The truth will make you even more conceited, therefore I shall stay silent out of consideration for your character. But what I'm marvelling at is the man's cheek.'

A huge weight seemed to have been lifted off Urmi's shoulders, one that she had been carrying for a long time. She could not decide how to celebrate the happiness of freedom. First, she tore up the reviled list of tasks. Then she flung her engagement ring out of the window towards the beggar in the lane outside.

'Can these thick books with all those passages underlined in pencil be sold to a hawker?'

'Suppose they can't, how will it matter?'

'What if a ghost from the past is living in there, waiting to appear by my bed to wag his finger at me?'

'If that's what you're worried about I'll buy them myself without bothering with the hawker.'

'What'll you do with them?'

'Give them a Hindu funeral. I'm ready to go to Gaya for the last rites if that will comfort you.'

'No, I can't take such excesses.'

'All right, I'll construct a pyramid in a corner of your library and turn them into mummies in it.'

'You're not going to work today.'

'Not at all?'

'Not at all.'

'What must I do?'

'We'll disappear in your car.'

'Get permission from your sister.'

'No, we'll come back and tell her, she'll scold me afterwards. I can survive that.'

'All right, I'm ready to accept your sister's scolding too. I won't be unhappy if we have a puncture. I don't even mind running over a couple of people at forty miles an hour and going to jail. But promise me, you'll come back to our house after our motoring odyssey.'

'I will, I will, I will!'

They returned to Bhawanipur after the motor trip, but their blood refused to flow slower than forty miles an hour. Every demand, every fear, every shame in their lives was left behind by this scorching pace.

For a few days, Shashanka's work was completely forgotten. He knew full well what he was doing was wrong. His business might even suffer badly. In bed, at night, his anxieties and apprehensions would assume even larger proportions. But the next day he was drunk again on his freedom, like Yaksha in Kalidasa's *Meghdoot**. Once you have had one drink, you have to have another to drown the remorse.

---

*Kalidasa's yaksha is exiled as punishment to Ramgiri. He longs for his freedom so he can be reunited wih his beloved.

125

Shashanka

SOME TIME WENT by this way. Shashanka was under a spell, his emotions ran deep.

It had taken some time for Urmi to understand herself clearly, but she was shocked when she did.

For some reason Urmi was afraid of Mathur-dada and used to avoid him. That morning, Mathur had gone into Sharmila's room, not emerging till the afternoon.

After he left, her sister sent for Urmi. Sharmila's expression was stern, though calm. 'I hope you know what you've done, disrupting his work every day.'

Urmi was stricken by dread. 'What is it, didi?' she asked.

'Mathur-dada has informed me that your brother-in-law has not been supervising his business personally for quite some time now.

'He had entrusted Jawaharlal with the responsibility, and Jawaharlal promptly began to pilfer supplies liberally. The roofs of the large godowns have turned out to be porous; after the rain the other day it was discovered that their bases are rotting away. Because of the reputation of our company they hadn't tested anything; now we have lost both credibility and profits. Mathur-dada is ending the partnership.'

Urmi's heart leapt into her mouth, her face turned ashen. The secret hidden in her heart was suddenly revealed to her as if in a flash of lighthing. She saw that she had been blind, unable to tell right from wrong. Shashanka's work had been her competitor, all her quarrels were with it. Urmi used to burn with the desire to wean him away from his work and hold him to herself. It had often happened that when visitors had come on work while Shashanka was in the bath, Urmi had carelessly instructed the servant, 'Tell them he can't see anyone now.'

She was worried that Shashanka would not have any time for her after his bath, that he would get so involved in his work that her day would amount to nothing. A horrifying picture of her addiction rose before her eyes.

She threw herself at her sister's feet, repeating in a choked voice, 'Send me away, throw me out of your home this instant.'

Sharmila had been determined not to forgive Urmi in any circumstances; but she melted.

Placing her hand gently on Urmimala's head, she said, 'Don't fret, we'll find a way out.'

Urmi sat up. 'Why should you be the one to lose all the money, didi?' she asked. 'I have some too, after all.'

'Are you mad?' answered Sharmila. 'It's not as if I don't have enough myself. I've told Mathur-dada not to make a fuss about this. I will make good his losses. And I'm telling you too, your brother-in-law mustn't get to know that I've come to know all this.'

'Forgive me, didi, forgive me,' said Urmi, repeatedly striking her forehead against her sister's feet.

Wiping her tears, Sharmila said tiredly, 'Who's the one that deserves forgiveness, my dear? The world is so complex. Dreams don't materialize, effort goes waste.'

Urmi didn't want to leave her sister's side for even a moment—she took over every responsibility, from giving Sharmila her medicine to bathing her, from feeding her to tucking her in at night. She even went back to her books, that too without leaving her sister's bedside. She trusted neither herself, nor Shashanka.

The outcome was that Shashanka visited the patient's room over and over again. Thanks to the natural blindness of the male, he did not realize that the significance was not lost on his wife, while Urmi died of shame. Shashanka tempted her with a Mohun Bagan football match, in vain. Unfolding a newspaper, he showed her Charlie Chaplin's name underlined in it, without any effect. While Urmi was not out of reach, Shashanka had at least tried to continue with his work, despite the temptation. Now even that became impossible.

Despite her grief Sharmila felt a certain enjoyment initially, at her hapless husband's attempts to pester Urmi. But gradually she saw that he was suffering greatly; he looked pale, he had dark circles under his eyes. Since Urmi no longer sat by his side during his meals, both his enthusiasm and his appetite were clearly on the wane. The wave of happiness that had washed over the house recently had now ebbed away completely, but the old lifestyle had not returned either.

Once Shashanka had been indifferent about his appearance. He would ask the barber for as close a crop as possible, so that he didn't have to use a comb. Having argued with him furiously over this, Sharmila had finally given up trying. But Urmi's succinct protests, accompanied by loud laughter, had not fallen on deaf ears. For the first time Shashanka's scalp tasted fragrant hair oil, and acquired a new hairstyle. But now the neglect of his hair only betrayed his agony. So much so that neither open nor secret giggles over this were acceptable. Sharmila's anxiety exceeded her unhappiness. Pity for her husband and reproach for herself ached within her breast, aggravating the pain caused by her illness.

The army from Fort William was scheduled to play war games at the Maidan. 'Would you like to go, Urmi?' asked Shashanka tentatively. 'I've got good seats.'

Sharmila spoke before Urmi could respond. 'Certainly she'll go. Of course she will. She's been dying to go out.'

Encouraged, Shashanka asked just a day or two later, 'The circus?'

Urmimala displayed nothing but eagerness at the proposal. And then, 'The Botanical Garden?'

This proved to be a stumbling block. Urmi wasn't willing to leave her sister alone too long.

Her sister herself sided with Shashanka. The man was worn out spending all his time with masons and bricklayers— all he did was labour in the grime and dust. He would collapse unless he could take a spin in the fresh air. By the same logic, a steamer trip to Rajganj wasn't unreasonable either. Sharmila reflected that her husband wouldn't be able to bear losing the person he had no qualms about losing his livelihood for.

While no one told Shashanka anything in as many words, he could sense implicit support from all directions. He had more or less convinced himself that Sharmila was feeling no particular pain, that she was happy enough to bring them together and see them happy with each other. It may not have been possible for any other woman, but then Sharmila was quite extraordinary. When Shashanka had been an employee in a firm, an artist had drawn a portrait of Sharmila's with colour pencils. It had been tucked away in his portfolio all this time. Pulling it out, he had it framed at a foreign store in great style and hung it on the wall of his office directly opposite his chair. The gardener put fresh flowers in the vase before it, every day.

Eventually, while showing Urmi how well the sunflowers were blooming in the garden, Shashanka suddenly took her hand, saying, 'I'm sure you know that I am in love with you. And as for your sister, she's a goddess. I have never revered anyone as much as I revere her. She isn't a mere mortal, she's on a far higher plane.'

Her sister had explained to Urmi repeatedly that her greatest comfort was that Urmi would be present even when she herself was gone. It pained her sister to even imagine another woman in this household—she couldn't bear to think of a situation so terrible that there wouldn't even be a woman to take care of Shashanka. Her sister had explained about the business too, saying that were his love to be thwarted the blow would ruin all his work as well. Once his heart was satiated, discipline would automatically be restored to his work.

Shashanka's heart was full of song. He now occupied a wondrous world, a delightful dream where no burden was heavier than a feather.

These days he was unwaveringly dedicated to observing the Sabbath on Sunday, like a faithful Christian. One day he told Sharmila, 'The jute mill owners have made their steam launch available for a day—since it's Sunday tomorrow, I'm thinking of taking Urmi out to Diamond Harbour early tomorrow morning, we'll be back by evening.'

Sharmila felt her veins being twisted, wrinkles of agony appeared on her forehead. Shashanka didn't even notice.

Sharmila merely enquired, 'What about food?'

'I've arranged it all with a restaurant,' answered Shashanka.

Once all this used to be Sharmila's responsibility, she would make the arrangements without bothering Shashanka. Now everything had been turned upside down. No sooner did Sharmila say, 'All right,' then Shashanka disappeared. Sharmila felt like weeping. 'Why am I still alive?' she kept asking herself, burying her face in her pillow.

It was their wedding anniversary that Sunday. The occasion had been celebrated every year without fail. This time too she had made all the arrangements without leaving her bed—and without informing her husband. The plan was simple; she would make Shashanka wear the red silk dhoti that he had worn for their wedding, while she herself would put on her wedding sari. Draping a garland around her husband's neck she would serve him a meal, light some incense, play the shehnai on the gramophone in the next room. Shashanka usually surprised her by buying her gifts he knew she would like.

'I'm sure he will this time too,' Sharmila had mused. 'I'll get to know tomorrow.'

She simply couldn't bear it that day; every time her room was empty she said out loud, 'Lies, all lies, why prolong this charade?' She couldn't sleep that night. At dawn she heard the car leave from the front door. 'You don't exist, God,' she sobbed.

From this point on her illness worsened rapidly. When the symptoms became particularly serious, she sent for her husband. It was evening, the room lights were dimmed, she signalled to the nurse to leave. Making her husband sit down by her side, she took his hand, saying, 'You are the gift I had sought from God. He did not give me the strength you deserve. I did as much as I could. I've made many mistakes, forgive me.'

Shashanka was about to speak, but she interrupted him. 'No, don't say anything. I'm leaving Urmi to you. She is my sister. You will discover me in her, you will discover many things you never received from me. No, be quiet, don't say anything. Only in my hour of death have I been fortunate enough to make you happy.'

'The doctor's here,' said the nurse outside the door.

'Send him in,' said Sharmila. The conversation ended there. Sharmila's uncle was an enthusiastic votary of all kinds of unorthodox medical treatment. He was currently engaged in serving a sage of some kind. When the doctors declared their inability to do anything more, he insisted that Sharmila try out a medicine provided by a seer returned from the Himalayas. Its ingredients were a ground Tibetan root and plenty of milk. Shashanka couldn't tolerate quacks of any kind. He objected vehemently. 'It may not help, but it will give mama* some comfort,' said Sharmila.

---

*Maternal uncle.

The potion provided instant results. Sharmila's breathing difficulties eased, her blood pressure dropped. A week passed, a fortnight passed; Sharmila sat up in bed again. The doctor claimed that imminent death sometimes galvanized the body into a desperate last-minute effort at survival. Sharmila survived.

'What is this!' she reflected. 'What do I do now? Will this second life prove to be worse than death?'

Meanwhile, Urmi was packing. Her sojourn here was over.

'You cannot leave,' said her sister.

'What do you mean?'

'Are you telling me a man has never married his wife's sister in Hindu society?'

'Shame!'

'Who cares for criticism! Is public opinion greater than the writ of destiny?'

Sending for Shashanka, she said, 'Let's move to Nepal. You were supposed to have got a job at the royal court there, you still can if you try. No one will protest there.' Sharmila didn't allow anyone room for hesitation. Preparations for their departure began immediately. But still Urmi wandered around miserably, keeping out of sight.

'Imagine my condition if you were to leave me now,' Shashanka told her.

'I cannot think any more,' Urmi replied. 'Whatever the two of you decide.'

It took some time to get things in order. When it was time to go, Urmi said, 'Wait another week, let me put things in order with kaka-babu, he's the manager of the estate, after all.' She left.

Mathur arrived to meet Sharmila, looking glum. 'You're leaving not a moment too soon,' he said. 'After you and I had settled things I had divided up the projects between Shashanka and myself. I didn't link his profit and loss to mine. Now that

132

he's winding up his work, Shashanka has been examining his accounts. It turns out that all your money has been sunk. And the debt that has piled up over and above can be only repaid by selling your house.'

'So close to bankruptcy—and he didn't get to know?' asked Sharmila. 'Bankruptcy is like a bolt of lightning, it doesn't announce itself even a moment before it strikes. He knew there were losses, things could still have been brought under control. But his judgement deserted him, he started speculating on the rocky coal market to make up for his losses quickly. What he bought high had to be sold low; and today he has suddenly realized all his money has been blown up like fireworks, leaving behind only the ashes. Now if by God's grace the job in Nepal materializes, things will be fine.'

Sharmila didn't fear poverty. On the contrary, she knew that scarcity would make her place in her husband's household more secure. She was confident that she could soften the blow of penury in their everyday life, especially since the jewellery she still owned would ensure they wouldn't have to suffer greatly. It had even occurred to her, albeit with reservations, that if Shashanka married Urmi her money would be his too. But daily sustenance was not everything.

The assets that her husband had built over all these years, with his own hands, his own efforts—respect for which had led Sharmila to set aside her strongest desires—had led her to expect a comfortable life; this had now vanished, like a mirage. The ignominy ground her to dust.

'If only I'd died then,' she told herself, 'I would have been spared this. Whatever fate had held for me has come true, but wouldn't the utter emptiness of abject poverty make him repent one day?' He might not be able to forgive the person whose allure so overwhelmed him that he allowed such a thing to happen; the food she served him might turn to ashes

133

in his mouth. Embarrassed by the outcome of his drunken behaviour, he would blame the wine. If they did have to depend on Urmi's property, his self-loathing would goad him to mistreat her.

Meanwhile, Shashanka had been made aware, while settling his accounts with Mathur, that Sharmila's entire investment in his business had been lost. Sharmila had not informed him; she had paid the money owed to Mathur, instead. He recollected that it was with a loan from Sharmila that he had expanded his business, after resigning from his job. Now that his business had failed he was returning to employment, still carrying the burden of his debt to Sharmila. He would never be able to shed this burden. How could he expect to repay the loan with a monthly salary?

They had about ten days to go, before leaving for Nepal. He hadn't been able to sleep all night. Tumbling out of bed at dawn, he smashed his fist down on the dressing table, announcing, 'Shan't go to Nepal!' He vowed, 'You and I shall live right here in Calcutta with Urmi—under the cruel gaze of a disapproving society. And I'm going to rebuild my business right here in Calcutta too.'

Sharmila was making a list of things to take and things to leave behind. Hearing him call her—'Sharmila! Sharmila!' —she dropped her notebook and went running into her husband's room. Fearing some sudden catastrophe, she asked with a quaking heart, 'What is it?'

'We shan't go to Nepal,' he told her. 'Shan't bother about society. We'll stay right here.'

'Why, what's the matter?' asked Sharmila.

'Work,' answered Shashanka.

That old chant—work. Sharmila's heart beat faster.

'Don't imagine I'm a coward, Sharmi. Can you even imagine I'd sink so low as to run away from my responsibilities?'

Going up to him, Sharmila took his hand. 'Explain to me what's happened.'

'I'm in debt to you again, don't try to hide it from me,' said Shashanka.

'All right, I won't,' said Sharmila.

'Just like before, I'm going to start repaying my debt. Today. I *shall* earn back everything that I've lost, I promise you. Put your faith in me again, like you did once.'

Leaning her head on her husband's chest, Sharmila said, 'Have faith in me too. Explain all your work to me, prepare me for it, teach me to be worthy of your work.'

'Letter,' came a cry from outside. Two letters arrived, both written in Urmi's hand. One of them was addressed to Shashanka.

I'm on my way to Bombay now. I'm going to England. I'm going to learn medicine there as my father wanted. It should take six or seven years. Whatever I have destroyed in your home will be restored on its own in time. Don't worry for me, it's you I shall be worrying for.

The letter for Sharmila…

…I erred without meaning to, forgive me. It will give me great joy if you say I haven't, I can hope for nothing more. Who knows what brings happiness ultimately? If I don't find it, so be it. It's better than making another mistake.

Malancha (1934)

The Arbour

She had been banished from the very garden that had claimed her heart, the heart of the childless mother. It was such a cruel separation..

One

THE PILLOWS WERE plumped up behind her back. Neeraja was propped up on them on her sickbed. A white silk sheet covered her legs like the pale light from a crescent moon in a cloudy sky. Her skin was pallid, her bangles limp, the veins a deep blue on her emaciated arms; even her thick eyelashes were touched by the shadow of sickness.

The floor was made of white marble, a framed portrait of Ramakrishna Paramhansa hung on the wall; besides the bed, a stool, two cane murrahs, and a clothes rack in the corner. There was no other furniture in the room. A brass pitcher in another corner held a bunch of tuberose flowers, their faint fragrance floating in the heavy air.

The window looking to the east was open. The orchid room, bordered by a straggling fence, was visible in the garden below; flowering vines wound around its pickets. A pump rumbled by the small lake nearby; the water gurgled as it flowed through the little canals alongside the flower beds. The cuckoo cooed in desperation, in the face of the heady scent of the mango orchard. The clock in the gatehouse marked the advent of afternoon, its chimes matching the strokes of the blinding sun. The gardeners were now off duty till three o'clock.

The chiming of the clock brought a pang to Neeraja's heart; she felt suddenly pensive. Ayah* arrived to shut the

---

*Nanny.

door. 'Leave it be!' Neeru said, gazing out to where the sunlight dappled the ground beneath the trees.

Her husband Aditya had made a name for himself in the flower trade. In their marriage, Neeraja and her husband had come together through tending to the garden. The flowers and blossoms, with their ever-changing loveliness, had always renewed their joy in each other. Just as the émigré awaits letters from friends back home on the days when the special post arrives, so too did they await, from season to season, the welcome of their flowers and plants.

That day Neeraja couldn't help but recall an image from the past. It wasn't all that long ago, but still it felt like history; from aeons ago, from across a vast continent. An ancient neem tree stood on the western side of the garden. It had had a partner in a similar tree, but that one had decayed and died a long time ago; they had chopped its trunk up into even pieces and made a small table from it. This was where they had had their morning cup of tea, sunlight filtering through the green boughs to cascade at their feet; birds and squirrels approaching them for crumbs. Then the pair would work on their garden together. Neeraja holding a silk parasol with a floral pattern above her head, and Aditya wearing a sola hat, garden shears slung from his waist.

When their friends visited, socializing merged with gardening. 'Really, I'm so jealous of your dahlias,' friends were frequently heard saying. 'Are those sunflowers?' others would ask, like amateurs. 'Oh no, those are marigolds,' Neeraja would answer, inordinately pleased. Someone had once asked knowledgeably—'How did you manage to grow such enormous jasmines, Neeraja Debi? You're a magician. They're as large as gardenias.' The connoisseur was rewarded; he took home five jasmines plants, complete with pots, inducing scowls on Hala the gardener's face. For days on end, Neeraja and Aditya would take their entranced friends on tours of the estate through the

140

flower gardens, the orchards, the vegetable patches. When they left Neeraja would give them baskets piled high with roses, magnolias, carnations—along with papaya, lemon, and wood apples, of course; the formidable wood apples of their garden. When the season was right, tender coconut juice was served at the end of the tour. 'How sweet it is,' the satiated guests would say. 'From our garden,' would be the answer. 'Ah, that explains it,' everyone would chorus.

She remembered the Darjeeling tea at dawn, whose vapours had carried the aromas of the seasons and now seemed to mingle with her sighs, and felt utterly desolate. From which bandit did she want to snatch back those golden days? Why was there no one for her rebellious heart to attack? She wasn't one to accept her fate without demur. Who was responsible for this? Who was this innocent whose writ ran all over the world? Who was it who had so meaninglessly succeeded in turning this perfection upside down?

Ten years had passed after her wedding, in pure bliss. Her friends envied her secretly, believed that she had got much more than her market price warranted. 'Lucky dog,' his friends had said to Aditya.

The tranquil waters of Neeraja's happiness were first disturbed by their pet Dolly. Before his wife had arrived, it was Dolly who was Aditya's companion in his solitary room. Eventually, her devotion was divided between the couple with Neeraja getting the lion's share. The moment she saw the car approach the main gate, Dolly would get upset, shaking her tail violently to signal her objection to their departure. She would jump into the car uninvited, her audacity only contained by her mistress's sternly raised index finger. Her tail tightly coiled in misery, she would lie slumped by the front door. When they were late, she would walk around sniffing at the air, filling the skies with her heart-rending question, asked in the inarticulate language of her species. But then Dolly was afflicted by an unknown disease. Casting heartbreaking glances at their faces, she died with her head on Neeraja's lap.

Neeraja's was a stubborn love. It was beyond her imagination, that anyone, even God, could intervene against it. All this while she had blindly believed that the world was on her side. Nothing had happened yet to shake that faith. But when it proved possible for Dolly to die, the first chink appeared in her armour. A door seemed to have opened up to misfortune. She felt that the lord and master of the universe was a disorderly soul—his apparent benevolence could no longer be relied on.

Everyone had lost hope of Neeraja having a child. They had given Ganesh a place to live in their establishment, and just as his young son was beginning to stir Neeraja's thwarted maternal passion—the boy reeling under its relentless onslaught—she became pregnant. The mother's soul flowered within her, the horizon ahead glowed pink in the dawn of new life; sitting beneath a tree Neeraja busied herself stitching clothes for the new born, producing a hundred different patterns.

Finally, it was time for the child to be delivered. The midwife realized a crisis was imminent. Aditya became so fretful that the doctor berated him into keeping his distance. The scalpel had to be wielded and the baby killed to save the mother. Neeraja could not even sit up after this. Like the river in summer reduced to a trickle on a bed of sand, she could only lie in her bed, anaemic, spent. She had exhausted her once plentiful life force.

The window before the bed was open; the warm breeze bore the scent of frangipani flowers—now and then a whiff of grapefruit—as though the distant days of her spring were asking her softly, 'How are you?'

What cut her to the quick was that Aditya's distant cousin Sarala had been sent for to help him tend to the garden.

142

Whenever she spotted Sarala through the open window, supervising the gardeners in a bonnet embroidered in silk, she simply couldn't come to terms with the uselessness of her own limbs. And yet she used to invite this very Sarala to the seeding ceremony each season when she was healthy. The work would begin at the crack of dawn. Afterwards, they would swim and bathe in the lake, then feast under the trees on rustic plates of plantain leaves, a gramophone playing Indian as well as Western music. The gardeners would be given their ration of curds, rice, and sweets. Their noisy conversations under the tamarind trees would be audible to everyone. Evening would approach gradually, the water on the lake would ripple under the late afternoon breeze, birds would sing on the boughs of the Spanish cherry tree, the day would end in happy exhaustion.

Why did her feelings, which used to flow so sweetly, have to have turned so bitter? Just as her present physical weakness was unfamiliar, so too was this strange barrenness that she now perceived in herself. There was no generosity in it. She recognized her own meanness clearly and felt ashamed, yet couldn't suppress it. She worried that Aditya might have noticed her small-mindedness. Some day soon, perhaps, he would see for himself that Neeraja's emotions were like a fruit damaged by the beak of a bat, unfit for human consumption.

The afternoon clock chimed. The gardeners left. The garden was deserted. Neeraja gazed into the distance. She saw not even a mirage of wild hope. Beneath the glare of the sun, emptiness seemed to follow emptiness, bereft of even a single shadow.

Two

'ROSHNI!' NEERAJA CALLED.

The ayah entered; middle-aged, with greying hair, a thick brass bangle on her sturdy wrist, a large scarf draped around her body above the long skirt. Her lean, rigid frame and shrivelled expression emanated an unshakeable harshness; as though she were sitting in judgement to deliver an unfavourable verdict against mankind. She had been the one who had raised Neeraja, and all her solicitude was centred on her. She was wary of—and hostile to—anyone who came near Neeraja, not even excluding her husband.

'Shall I get you a glass of water, khnokhi*?' she asked, still referring to Neeraja, in her country accent, as a little girl.

'No. Sit down here.' The ayah sat on the floor, drawing her knees up.

Neeraja wanted to talk, and the ayah was the vessel of her outpourings.

'I heard the front door open early this morning,' said Neeraja.

Roshni said nothing; but the irritation on her face clearly said, 'And what's new about that?'

'So he took Sarala with him into the garden?' Neeraja asked needlessly.

---

*Rustic form of Bengali for khuki, meaning little girl.

She knew the answer perfectly well, but still she asked every day. The ayah grimaced, gesturing with her hand to signal the futility of the query.

Looking away, Neeraja spoke to herself. 'He used to wake me up at dawn too, I used to go with him to work in the garden too, at that same hour. It wasn't so very long ago.'

She wasn't expected to enter this discussion, but the ayah couldn't contain herself. 'As if the garden would have dried up without her,' she said.

'Not a day went by without my sending the morning batch of flowers to New Market,' Neeraja continued, under her breath. 'There was a batch this morning too, I heard the cart. Who looks after the dispatch these days, Roshni?'

The ayah pursed her lips, without providing the answer that Neeraja already knew.

'At least the gardeners couldn't cheat as long as I was there,' Neeraja told her.

'Those days are gone,' the ayah said bristling. 'It's daylight robbery now.'

'Really?'

'Would I lie to you? How much of the flowers do you suppose actually get to New Market in Calcutta? As soon as jamai-babu* leaves, the gardeners set up shop outside the back door.'

'Doesn't anyone stop them?'

'Who cares?'

'Why don't you tell jamai-babu?'

'Who am I to tell him? I must stay in my place. Why don't you tell him? It's all yours, after all.'

'Let it go on this way, let it. After some more time, when they've finished it all off, they'll be found out. One day they'll

---

*Term of address for the son-in-law by the wife's family, usually by the younger generation.

realize the difference between the mother's love and the stepmother's. Don't say a word to them.'

'But I have to say, khnokhi, that gardener of yours, Hala, is useless.'

Hala's disinterest in work wasn't the only reason for Roshni's annoyance; more importantly, Neeraja was becoming unduly fond of him.

'I don't blame the gardeners,' said Neeraja. 'Why should they stand for a new mistress? They've been gardeners for generations, and the new lady of the house has got her learning from books, she isn't worthy of ordering them around. Hala doesn't want to follow meaningless orders, he complains to me. I tell him not to bother, and not to say a word.'

'Jamai-babu wanted to dismiss him the other day.'

'Why, whatever for?'

'He was smoking while a cow from was munching on the plants. "Why don't you shoo the cow away?" jamai-babu asked him. He answered right back, "You expect me to shoo away cows? It's the cows who chase me. I'm scared for my life!"'

Neeraja smiled at this, saying, 'That's the way he talks. No matter what, he's my protégé.'

'It's because of you that jamai-babu puts up with him, whether it's cows marauding in the garden or rhinos rampaging in the backyard. I still have to say, it's not good to be so demanding.'

'Keep quiet, Roshni. I know perfectly well why he couldn't be roused to chase away the cow. He's burning up inside. Isn't that Hala with the gamchha wrapped around his head? Call him quickly.'

Haladhar the gardener entered, in response to the ayah's summons.

'Well? Are you following new orders these days?'

'Of course!' said Hala. 'They make me laugh, and they make me cry too.'

'What kind of orders?'

'I'm supposed to fetch rocks and stones from where the Mullicks' house is being demolished and spread them out beneath the trees. That's her order. I said, "When the sun is strong, the heat from the rocks will damage the trees." She pays no attention to me.'

'Why don't you tell babu about it?'

'I did. He shouted at me, told me to keep my mouth shut. Let me go, boudidi*, I can't take this any more.'

'I know, I saw you with a basket full of rubble.'

'You're my lifelong mistress, boudidi. She's shamed me in your presence. I'm going to lose face before all my people now. Have I been reduced to a porter?'

'All right, you can go now. If that didimoni of yours asks you to carry rubble again tell her I said no. Why aren't you going?'

'I got a letter—the cow we use for farming back home has died.' He proceeded to scratch his head.

'No she hasn't died, she's alive and well,' said Neeraja. 'Here's two rupees, and not another word out of you.' Taking the money out of the brass box on the stool, she gave it to him. 'Now what?' she added.

'One of your old saris for my wife. Everyone will sing your praises.' He grinned widely, displaying teeth stained black with paan.

'Give him that sari there on the rack, Roshni,' Neeraja directed.

'What do you mean, that's your Dhaka silk sari,' protested Roshni, shaking her head vehemently.

'So what if it is? They're all the same to me these days. As if I'll ever get a chance to put it on.'

---

*Traditional form of address for one's brother's (or male cousin's) wife. Also used for senior married women.

'Nothing doing,' said Roshni, with a determined expression. 'I can give him that mill-made sari of yours with the red border. Look Hala, if you're going to bother khnokhi this way I'm telling babu to get rid of you.'

Hala grabbed Neeraja's knees and started whining. 'Fate has turned against me, boudidi.'

'What's the matter with you now?'

'I think of ayah-ji as my aunt. My mother is dead, all this while I thought ayah-ji actually loved me. Then why does she have to come in the way just as you're feeing generous? It's nobody's fault but my fate's. Why else would you have to fall sick and hand over Hala to someone else's authority!'

'Not to worry, your aunt does love you. She was saying good things about you just a moment ago. Give him that sari, Roshni, or else he's going to picket here the rest of the day.'

With a sour expression, the ayah flung the sari at Hala. Gathering it up, he made an elaborate show of grateful deference. Rising to his feet, he said, 'I'd better wrap it in that towel. My hands are dirty, I might stain it.' Without waiting for approval, he took a towel off the clothes-stand, bundled the sari up in it and exited rapidly.

'Are you sure, Roshni, that jamai-babu's gone out?' Neeraja asked the ayah.

'I saw him leave myself. He was in such a hurry, he forgot his hat.'

'For the first time he forgot my regular morning flowers. It'll get worse day by day. And finally I'll be consigned to the rubbish heap of my own home, where they throw the burnt pieces of charcoal.'

Sarala approached. When she saw who was coming, the ayah grimaced and left.

Sarala entered the room holding an orchid. The flower was ivory-coloured, traces of violet at the edge of its petals, like an enormous butterfly with its wings spread out. She was slim and tall, her complexion on the dark side; the first thing you noticed about her were her large eyes, bright and sad. She had on a coarse handloom sari, her hair was done up carelessly, cascading over her shoulder in slow waves. Her blossoming beauty shorn of all adornment gave her appearance a look of carelessness.

Neeraja didn't look at her, Sarala deposited the flower gently on her bed.

'Who asked you to bring flowers?' Neeraja didn't try to hide her irritation.

'Adit-da*.'

'Why didn't he come himself?'

'He had to go to the New Market shop immediately after his morning cup of tea.'

'What's the rush?'

'The office was burgled last night.'

'Couldn't he make an effort to spare even five minutes?'

'You were in so much pain last night, you couldn't go to sleep till dawn. He came up to your door and went back, he told me to give you this flower if he wasn't back by the afternoon.'

Before starting his work for the day, Aditya always left a hand-picked flower by his wife's bedside. Neeraja had waited for it every single day. And now Aditya had chosen to send the day's special flower with Sarala. It hadn't occurred to him that the best part was giving the flower to her personally; even the holiest of water loses its appeal when it flows through the tap.

Pushing the flower aside disdainfully, Neeraja said, 'Have you any idea how much this would cost in the market? Send it to the shop, why waste it here?' Her voice choked.

Sarala understood. Realizing, too, that answering would only increase Neeraja's anguish, not lighten it, she waited in silence.

---

*Da is a shortened form of dada, meaning elder brother.

'Do you know the name of this flower?' Neeraja asked needlessly, a little later.

Sarala could easily have said she didn't, but her pride was hurt, so she answered, 'Amaryllis.'

'Fat lot you know!' Neeraja cut her down in unfair rage. 'It's called Grandiflora.'

'Maybe,' answered Sarala softly.

'What do you mean maybe? It is! Are you suggesting I'm wrong?'

Sarala knew Neeraja had deliberately used an incorrect name to register her protest; needling someone else to forget her own hurt. Admitting defeat, she was slowly on her way out when Neeraja called her back. 'Wait. What were you doing all morning, where were you?'

'In the orchid room.'

'Why do you need to go in there so often?' Neeraja asked, in agitation.

'Adit-da told me to make cuttings from the old orchids for new ones.'

'You'll bungle the whole thing like a novice. I've trained Hala personally, couldn't you have asked him to do it?' Neeraja admonished her.

There could be no rejoinder. The honest answer was that Hala did the work perfectly under Neeraja's supervision but not under Sarala's. In fact, he deliberately humiliated her with his indifference. The gardener had surmised—correctly— that incompetence under the new regime would keep the old regime happy. It was as though it was more worthwhile to boycott classes and fail the exams than to get a degree.

Sarala could have lost her temper, but she did not. She knew boudidi was aching inside. She had been banished from the very garden—so near and yet so far—that had claimed her heart, the heart of the childless mother. It was such a cruel separation.

'Shut it, shut that window,' Neeraja commanded.

Shutting it, Sarala asked, 'Shall I bring your orange juice?'

'No I don't need anything, you may go now.'

'It's time for the tonic,' Sarala said, apprehensively.

'I don't want any tonic. Have you been told to do anything else in the garden?'

'I have to plant some rose stems.'

'So he considers this to be the right time of the year,' Neeraja scoffed. 'Who on earth came up with this idea, I wonder.'

'There's been a sudden increase in orders from small towns, so he's decided to grow more plants somehow or other before the next monsoon. I tried to stop him.'

'Oh, you tried to stop him! All right, send Hala to me.'

The gardener arrived. 'Now you've become too good to plant rose trees yourself! Is didimoni* your assistant? Plant as many of them as you can before babu returns, no breaks for any of you today. Prepare the soil by the lake, use a mixture of sand with burnt foliage.' She decided that she would have a rose garden without leaving her bed. There would be no respite for Hala.

'I got a brass pot for you, boudidi,' Hala said unexpectedly, his face suffused by an indulgent smile. 'Made by Harasundar Maiti from Cuttack. You're the only one who can appreciate things like these. It'll make a lovely flower vase for you.'

'How much is it?' asked Neeraja.

'Never,' said Hala, sticking the tip of his tongue out in horror. 'How can I ask you to pay for it? I may be poor, but I'm not a beast. I owe my livelihood to you.'

Putting the gift down on the stool, he proceeded to transfer flowers into it from another vase. About to leave,

---

*A variation of didi, meaning elder sister used sometimes as endearment or to show subservience, as in this case.

after he was done, he turned back to say, 'You remember about my niece's wedding, don't you? Don't forget the bracelet, if I gift brass jewellery it's you they'll say bad things about. A gardener working for such a well-known family, a wedding in his family, everyone back home is watching.'

'All right, don't worry, you can go now.'

Hala left. Turning on her side, Neeraja put her head on her pillow and moaned, 'Roshni, Roshni, I've become petty too! Just like Hala, no better.'

'No khnokhi, how can you say that?' the ayah protested.

Neeraja continued, talking to herself. 'Fate! First it humiliates me before the world, then it humiliates me before myself. I know very well what Hala thinks of me these days. He played his games with me and is now laughing, having got his gifts. Fetch him here, I'll give him what he deserves—I have to fix his wicked ways once and for all.'

When the ayah rose to summon Hala, Neeraja said, 'Never mind, not today.'

Three

A LITTLE LATER her husband's cousin Ramen arrived to say, 'Dada sent me, boudi. He's tied up with work at the office, he'll eat at a restaurant, he'll be late getting back home.'

'You came all this way on the pretext of carrying a message, thakurpo? Is the office boy dead?'

'What pretext do I need besides you to come to you, boudi? And what does the office boy know of the messenger's real role?'

'Pearls before swine, my dear. Are you here because you lost your way? Your beloved is all alone in the lemon orchard, go pay her a visit.'

'I'd prefer to pay tribute first to the forest goddess; I'll go looking for the beloved afterwards.' Taking a novel out of his pocket, Ramen handed it to Neeraja.

'*Chain of Tears!*' said a pleased Neeraja. 'Just the book I was looking for. May the goddess of your garden be bound to your breast forever in chains of joy—she whom you refer to as your partner in your imagination, your consort in your dreams. Such amour, my dear.'

'I'm going to ask you something, boudi,' said Ramen, suddenly. 'Answer me honestly.'

'Ask me what?'

'Did you fight with Sarala today?'

'What makes you ask?'

'I saw her sitting all by herself on the steps by the lake. But women aren't shirkers by nature like men are. I've never seen Sarala so distracted. "Where's your mind today?" I asked. "Gone with the searing wind that blows the dry leaves away," she replied. "That's a riddle," I said. "Tell me in simple words." "Must everything be explained in words?" she answered. Another riddle. I remembered that line from the song, "Whose words have hurt you?"'

'Maybe your cousin's.'

'Impossible! Dada is a man, you see. He may scream at your gardener, but quarrel with the flowers? Out of the question!'

'Enough of your nonsense. I have a serious request, you have to keep it. Marry Sarala, I beg of you. Delivering her from an unmarried life will be one of your good deeds.'

'I don't hanker after good deeds but I do hanker after her, I swear to you.'

'What's the problem then? She has a heart, doesn't she?'

'I haven't even asked. I told you, she'll remain my partner in my imagination, never in real life.'

Suddenly clutching Ramen's hands fervently, Neeraja said, 'Why not, she *has* to. I *shall* see the two of you married before I die, else I promise to haunt both of you as a ghost.'

Her intensity surprised Ramen. Shaking his head, he said finally, 'Boudi, by marriage you may be my senior, but actually I'm older. Stray winds bring nothing but weeds; ignore them and they take root, no one can dislodge them after that.'

'Don't preach to me. I'm your senior in the family, I'm advising you to get married. Don't put it off. There are auspicious dates this coming March.'

'Any date is auspicious for me. But even if there are dates, there's no way. I've been to jail once, I haven't managed to get off the slippery road that leads back into it. The love god's soldiers don't patrol that path.'

'As if women fear jail these days!'

'Maybe they don't, but that's not the road to marriage. On that road, strength comes not from having your bride by your side, but in your heart. Let her stay there forever.'

Sarala entered, placed a glass of Horlicks on the stool and made to leave. 'Don't go,' said Neeraja. 'Come here, Sarala, do you know whose photograph this is?'

'Mine, of course,' said Sarala.

'An old photograph of yours,' replied Neeraja. 'When Aditya and you worked in your uncle's garden. You were probably about fifteen. You'd put on your sari the way Marathi women do, tucked between your legs.'

'Where did you get this?'

'I had seen it in his desk but hadn't noticed it. I had it fetched today. Sarala is much prettier now than back then, thakurpo. Don't you think so?'

'Was there a Sarala in existence at all then? I didn't know any, at any rate. Today's Sarala is the only truth for me. Whom should I compare her to?' Ramen said.

'She is full of mysterious intensity today—like a heavy cloud about to burst forth with rain. Isn't this what you people call romantic, thakurpo?'

Sarala was about to leave; Neeraja told her, 'Stay a while, Sarala. Let me look at her through a man's eyes, thakurpo. Tell me the first thing you notice about her.'

'All of her,' said Ramen.

'I'm sure it's her eyes; she knows how to make them sort of deep. No, don't leave, Sarala. Stay a little longer. Her body is well shaped and flawless too.'

'Are you trying to auction her, boudi? You know very well my interest is already soaring.'

'Have you seen Sarala's hands, thakurpo, as perfectly formed and tender as they're strong and just as graceful,' Neeraja exclaimed with the enthusiasm of an agent. 'Have you ever seen anything like them?'

'It would be rude to give an answer to your face,' Ramen said smiling.

'Aren't you going to claim ownership of such lovely hands?'

'Maybe I won't make a claim for a lifetime, but I do make my claim every now and then. When I come to your room for a cup of tea, the magic of that hand turns it into much more than just a cup of tea. If accepting something from that hand and asking for it have something in common, that's enough for poor old me.'

Sarala rose to her feet from her stool. As she attempted to leave, Ramen blocked her way, saying, 'I'll let you go only if you promise me something.'

'What, tell me.'

'It's a full moon night. The traveller will arrive at your arbour. Even if there are things one can say, there will be no need to. There's a famine in the land, I haven't got my fill of you. Offering me one unexpected glimpse in this room is like throwing me a crumb my way—not acceptable. I want to find fulfilment tonight, slowly, not hurriedly, beneath that tree of yours.'

'All right, come then,' said Sarala, without any reserve.

'Then I'm off, boudi,' said Ramen, returning to Neeraja's bedside.

'You needn't stay any more. Boudi's done with what she had to do.'

Ramen departed.

Four

After Ramen left, Neeraja remained in bed, her face buried in her hands. Once she too had experienced such a stirring of the soul, turning many a spring night tumultuous. Unlike most women, she wasn't part of the furniture in her husband's household. She couldn't help recalling, as she lay in bed, how often her husband had wound a lock of her hair round his fingers saying to her passionately, 'You're my lovely wine girl in my hall of pleasure.'

Ten years had passed but the colours had not faded; the cup was just as full. Her husband would say to her, 'In ancient times trees used to flower at the touch of women's feet, flowers used to bloom at a taste of the shower from their lips; my garden has returned to that era of Kalidasa. Flowers have bloomed, in all their myriad hues, on either side of the path on which you walk, the rose garden is drunk on the wine you've sprinkled in the spring breeze.' Every now and then he would say, 'Without you this heaven of flowers would have been overrun by the invasion of monstrous traders. How fortunate for me that you are the queen of my heavenly arbour.' But why had her attraction dulled if she was still desirable? No wonder the queen couldn't occupy her throne today; earlier, she had not felt the least bit threatened. Her position had been unchallenged, she had been like the daily sunrise, the only orb in her husband's sky. Who could have guessed her position would be usurped so prematurely? Today her faith in herself was shaken, even the hint of doubt gave her tremors.

How else could Sarala have sprung from nowhere, with all her airs? Even someone like her could make Neeraja insecure today. After bestowing so much happiness, such glory on her for so many years, the Almighty had finally sneaked in like a common thief to steal those riches.

'Roshni, can you come here?'

'Yes, khnokhi.'

'Once upon a time your jamai-babu used to call me the queen of his pleasure palace. We've been married ten years— the colours haven't faded, but what of the palace?'

'Your palace hasn't run away anywhere, everything's fine. You didn't sleep all night, it's time you slept a little now. Let me massage your feet.'

'It's almost full moon night, isn't it? We spent many such nights without sleep, walking around our garden. How different these sleepless nights are from those. Now I'm dying for sleep, but where is that accursed sleep?'

'Just be quiet for a while, sleep will come on its own.'

'Do they walk around the garden in the moonlight?'

'I've seen them picking flowers for the morning dispatch. Where's the time for a promenade?'

'The gardeners are fast asleep, are they? So they don't like waking them up?'

'Who dares say anything to them in your absence?'

'Was that the carriage?'

'Yes, that's babu's carriage.'

'Give me the hand mirror, get the large rose from the vase. I look very pale today. Where's the box of safety pins? Go now.'

'I'm going, but you haven't touched your barley either— drink up, dear.'

'Won't touch it.'

'You've missed two doses of the medicine.'

'Stop nagging, go now, open the window before you go.'

The ayah left.

The clock struck three, the sunlight turned crimson, the shadows lengthened to the east, a breeze sprang up from the south, the lake looked as if it were going to flow over. The gardeners returned to work. Neeraja observed them as closely as she could from a distance.

Aditya arrived with quick footsteps, holding an armful of local saffron laburnums complete with their boughs. He heaped them over her feet. Sitting down on the bed, he clasped her hands. 'It's been so long since I saw you last, Neeru.'

Neeraja could no longer contain herself; she broke out in sobs. Alighting from the bed, Aditya knelt on the floor and embraced her, kissing her wet cheeks and saying, 'I'm sure you knew it wasn't my fault.'

'How would I know for sure? Things are no longer the same.'

'There's no need for such comparisons. You're still mine, just like before.'

'I'm afraid of everything these days. I have no confidence.'

'You enjoy this anxiety don't you? You just want to provoke me with a barb or two. Natural feminine cunning.'

'And isn't it natural for men to forget?'

'Do you even give me a chance to forget?'

'Don't say that, don't—the damned Lord has cursed me to ensure you get plenty of opportunities for it.'

'Wrong. You can only forget when you're happy, never when you're suffering.'

'Tell me the truth, didn't you forget this morning when you went off?'

'How can you say that. I *had* to go, but I felt awful till I returned.'

'Is that any way to sit? Put your feet up on the bed now.'

'You want to fence me in so I can't run away?'

'Yes, I do. Your feet will remain under my custody in life and in death.'

'You must suspect me now and then, that makes your love taste better.'

'No, I shan't. Not even a whiff of suspicion. Has a woman ever had a husband like you? Suspecting you would only mean shaming myself.'

'Then let me suspect *you*, or where's the excitement.'

'Go ahead, I'm not afraid. It'll be a farce.'

'Now I know you were angry with me.'

'Don't bring that up again. You needn't pronounce a sentence—doing what I did was punishment enough.'

'What sentence? If the heat of anger never rises it can only mean the pulse of love beats no more.'

'If I am ever angry with you mistakenly, remember this— it won't be me, but some evil spirit who's possessed me.'

'We all have our evil spirits, every now and then they rear their heads unprovoked. If good sense prevails we can invoke the name of God, the spirit flees.'

The ayah entered. 'Khnokhi hasn't had her milk, hasn't had her medicines, hasn't had her massage since morning. We can't tolerate such behaviour,' she said and flounced off, arms swinging.

'Now should I be angry with you?' asked Aditya, sprang to his feet the moment he heard this.

'Yes, do, be very angry, as angry as you can be, I've been bad—but forgive me afterwards.'

'Sarala, Sarala,' Aditya went to the door and called out.

Neeraja's nerves began to jangle. The thorn embedded in her flesh seemed to move in a little deeper.

Sarala arrived.

'Neeru hasn't had her medicine—hasn't she been given anything to eat either all day?' asked an annoyed Aditya.

'Don't scold her,' Neeraja intervened. 'It's not her fault. I was naughty and didn't have my food and medicines, scold me instead. Go away, Sarala, why should you get an unnecessary scolding?'

'What do you mean go away, let her bring you the medicine. Let her get you some Horlicks and milk.'

'Not fair, you already make her slave like a gardener all day, and now a nurse too. Don't you feel any sympathy at all? Why can't you call the ayah?'

'Can she do all this properly?'

'It's hardly a chore. She'll do it even better.'

'But…'

'No buts. Ayah, ayah!'

'Don't get so worked up. Do you want something awful to happen?'

'I'll send the ayah,' Sarala said and left. She couldn't even summon up a protest to what Neeraja had said. Aditya was surprised, wondering whether Sarala was indeed being made to work too hard.

After the medicines and other tasks were attended to, Aditya told the ayah, 'Fetch Sarala-didi.'

'Why do you need Sarala-didi for every little thing, you're going to drive the poor thing mad.'

'We have an important discussion.'

'Never mind the important discussion now.'

'It won't take long.'

'Sarala is only a woman, what important discussion can you have with her? Talk to Hala instead.'

'Ever since I married you, I've learnt that it's women who are efficient; men who are useless. We work out of compulsion, you work out of passion. I'm planning a thesis on this subject; there's no dearth of examples in my diary.'

'What words of condemnation shall I use for the god who has deprived just such a woman of her work? My mountain of labour has crumbled in an earthquake, that's why ghosts have taken over this dilapidated house.'

Sarala arrived. 'Has all the work in the orchid room been done?' asked Aditya.

'Yes, it has,' said Sarala.

'All of it?'

'All of it.'

'And the rose cuttings?'

'The gardeners are preparing the soil.'

'The soil! But I've prepared it already. If you expect Hala to take the responsibility, all you'll get are toothpicks.'

'Can you make some orange juice, Sarala,' Neeraja intervened quickly. 'Put some ginger and honey in it.'

Sarala left the room, her head bowed.

'Did you wake up at dawn today, like we used to?' asked Neeraja.

'Yes, I did.'

'Did you set the alarm as before?'

'Of course I did.'

'That old tree trunk? Were the tea things on it? Did Basu lay it all out properly?'

'He did. Or else I'd have filed a complaint in your court for dereliction of duty.'

'Both the stools laid out?'

'They were, just like before. The orange cups and saucers with the blue borders were laid out too; the silver milk jug, the white porcelain bowl of sugar, and the Japanese tray with the dragon.'

'Why did you keep the other stool empty?'

'Not by choice. The stars were all present in the sky, only the full moon remained beyond the horizon. I'd have summoned it if I could.'

'Why don't you ask Sarala to join you for your morning tea?'

He could easily have said, 'Because I can't bear to have anyone else take your place.' But instead, Mr Truthful said, 'I believe she's deep in prayers at that hour, she's not a godless heathen like me after all.'

'You took her to the orchid room after your morning tea today, didn't you?'

'Yes, there were things to be done, I explained it all to her and then rushed off to the shop.'

'I want to ask you something. Why don't you get Sarala and Ramen married?'

'Am I a professional matchmaker?'

'No, I'm not joking. Since she *has* to get married, will there be a more suitable boy than Ramen?'

'We have the boy on one side, the girl on the other, but I haven't had the chance to find out if there are hearts in between. That's where the stumbling block seems to be.'

'There would have been no stumbling block if you'd really been interested,' said Neeraja acidly.

'Two other people will get married, but I'm the one who has to be interested—is that how things work? Why don't you try?'

'Give her some respite from the flowers and bushes, her eyes will automatically seek out their destination.'

'Lovelight in the eyes can see through all the trees and mountains in the world. It's a sort of X-ray.'

'Rubbish. The truth is, you don't want this wedding to take place.'

'You've hit the nail on the head at last. Can you imagine what will happen to my garden if Sarala gets married? I have to think of my profit and loss too, don't I? What's the matter, has the pain returned?'

Aditya grew anxious.

'Nothing's the matter,' said Neeraja, brusquely. 'You don't have to worry about me.'

As her husband was readying to leave, she said, 'I hope you haven't forgotten that the orchid room was started just after our wedding. We made that room what it is together, the two of us, one day at a time. Doesn't it hurt you a bit to have it destroyed?'

'What on earth do you mean?' said Aditya in surprise. 'When did you see me hankering to have it destroyed?'

'What does Sarala know of growing flowers?' Neeraja asked him, agitated.

'What! How can you say that! Of course Sarala knows! The uncle who brought me up is her father's brother. You know very well that it was in his garden that I learnt the ropes. Meshomashai* used to say it is women who should grow flowers and milk cows, she was his assistant throughout.'

'And so were you.'

'Of course I was. But I had to read for my college exams, I couldn't devote as much time to it as she could. Meshomashai trained her personally.'

'It was the garden that was the ruin of your uncle. That's how positive her influence is. That's why I'm afraid. She brings bad luck. Haven't you noticed how wide her forehead is, how she prances about like a horse! It isn't good for a woman to think like a man. It makes bad things happen.'

'What's the matter with you today, Neeru! What on earth are you saying? Meshomashai knew how to grow flowers, not how to grow a business. Nobody could beat him when it came to a garden, nor when it came to losing money. He earned fame, but not profits. When he gave me the capital to invest in my own garden, I didn't have the faintest idea that his own funds were all but sunk. My only consolation is that I paid it all back before he died.'

---

*Mother's sister's husband—maternal uncle.

164

Sarala brought the orange juice. 'Put it there,' said Neeraja. Sarala obeyed and left. The glass remained untouched.

'Why didn't you marry Sarala?'

'Listen to you! The thought never even crossed my mind.'

'Never even crossed your mind? Is that how far your poetic feelings go?'

'My poetic feelings appeared for the first time when I saw you. Before that we were just a couple of savages living under the shadow of the forest, forgetting ourselves. I can't say what may have happened had we been brought up in today's culture.'

'What're you blaming culture for?'

'Today's culture is to strip the heart like Draupadi was stripped of her clothes. It forces you to be crudely physical before you learn to sense things. The hint of fragrance is too subtle; the only form of enquiry is tearing off the petals.'

'But Sarala isn't ugly.'

'I knew Sarala as Sarala, nothing else. Whether she was pretty or ugly was irrelevant.'

'Tell me the truth, didn't you love her?'

'Of course I loved her. Am I devoid of all feelings? How could I not love her? Meshomashai's son is a barrister in Rangoon, he needs no looking after. Meshomashai's lifelong wish was that Sarala tend to his garden. In fact he was sure that the garden alone would occupy her heart and soul; that she wouldn't ever want to marry. Then he was gone, Sarala was orphaned, creditors claimed the garden. I was heartbroken when it happened, dont you remember? She's mine to love, how can I not love her? I remember so well how full of laughter and liveliness Sarala used to be. She seemed to walk like a bird in flight. Today she carries such a burden in her heart and yet she hasn't collapsed. Not for a day has she come to me with a sigh, she's never even given herself the opportunity.'

'Stop now, I've heard enough about her from you, I don't need to hear any more,' interrupted Neeraja. 'Extraordinary woman. That's why I told you to make her the headmistress of the girls' school in Barasat. They've requested for this so many times.'

'The girls' school in Barasat? Why not the Andamans?'*

'No, it's not a joke. You can let Sarala work anywhere else in the garden but not in the orchid room.'

'But why not?'

'Sarala doesn't understand orchids, that's what I'm telling you.'

'And I'm telling you that she understands them even better than I do. My uncle's main interest was in orchids. He sent people off to get him orchids from the Celebes, Java, even from China. There was no one at the time who knew what they were worth.'

Neeraja knew this and that was why it was unpalatable to her.

'All right, fine, so she understands them far better than I do, even better than you do. Even so, I maintain that the orchid room is just yours and mine, she has no right to be there. Give her your entire garden if you really want to; just keep a tiny part of it dedicated to my memory alone. Surely I can stake this small claim after so many years together. It's my lot to be bedridden today, but does that mean... ' She couldn't speak any more; burying her face in her pillow, she began to sob in turmoil.

Aditya was stunned—as though he had been living in a dream all this time and was now jolted into wakefulness. What *was* this! He realized the tears had been a long time in the making. Neeraja's pain had built up to a crescendo, and he had no idea of it. He had been obtuse enough to imagine

---

*The British often dispatched Indian freedom fighters to prison in the Andaman Islands.

that she was happy that Sarala was able to take care of the garden. Sarala had no match when it came to making beautiful seasonal flower beds.

Suddenly he recalled that when he had praised Sarala for something recently declaring, 'I for one wouldn't have been able to set up a border of orange jasmines so perfectly,' Neeraja had said with a sharp laugh, 'If you pay a person more than they're worth, sir, you end up doing them harm.' Aditya recollected that if Neeraja ever managed to catch Sarala out over a mistake concerning flowers, she would point it out over and over again with loud gusts of laughter. He remembered clearly how Neeraja would look up unusual names of obscure flowers in English books; she would then ask Sarala to identify them, and when Sarala got one wrong, laugh uproariously. 'Some wizard you are, everyone knows it's called the Casseia javanica. Even Hala would have known.'

Aditya pondered the whole matter for quite a while. Then, taking Neeraja's hand he said, 'Don't cry any more, Neeru, tell me what I should do. Do you want Sarala not to be involved in the garden?'

Snatching her hand away Neeraja said, 'Nothing, I want nothing, it's your garden. You can ask anyone you want to look after it, what do I care.'

'Neeru, how could you say it's my garden alone. Isn't it yours too? When did we become separated from each other?'

'Ever since you got everything in the world, while I was left with just a corner in this room. How will this broken spirit of mine allow me to stand up to your amazing Sarala? Where do I have the power to look after you, to take care of your garden?'

'But Neeru, you've sent for Sarala so many times earlier, taken her advice. Don't you remember, just a couple of years ago, how both of you grafted the new pomelo on the old columban lemon to surprise me?'

'She wasn't so full of herself then. God has darkened my half of the world, that's why she's so, important to you now; she knows this and she knows that, you're nowhere as good when it comes to orchids as she is. I never heard any of this back then. Why then did you have to compare us during my dark hours? How can I compete with her today? How can I measure up to her?'

'Neeru, I feel utterly unprepared to hear the things you're telling me. You don't sound like my Neeru at all.'

'No, my dear, I'm the same Neeru. You haven't understood her even after all these years. That is my biggest punishment. Since we've been married, I have come to realize that your garden is as precious to you as your heart; I considered the garden no different from myself ever since. Or else I'd have quarrelled bitterly with your garden and I'd never have been able to bear it. It would have been my rival in love. You know how I have merged it within myself. How I have become one with it.'

'Of course I do. Everything I have is gathered within you.'

'Don't lie. Now I know there's someone else who can go into the garden whenever she wants to. It did not hurt you at all. Could you have even imagined slicing up my body and planting someone else's heart in it? Is the garden any less than my body? Would I ever have done such a thing?'

'What would you have done?'

'Shall I tell you? Maybe the garden would have been destroyed, the business gone bankrupt. I would have hired ten gardeners instead of one before I let in another woman, especially someone who's full of airs and graces—who thinks she knows more about tending to gardens than I do. Now that I am about to die, now that I no longer have the strength to prove myself, are you going to humiliate me every day with her arrogance? Shall I tell you how this could possibly have happened?'

168

'Yes, do.'

'Because you love her more than you love me. You concealed it all these years.'

Aditya remained seated, his head buried in his hands. Then he spoke, overcome. 'You've known me for ten years, Neeru, for better or for worse, in sickness and in health. If you can still say what you did, I am not going to respond. I'm going now. You'll get worse if I remain near you. I'll be in the Japanese room. Send for me when you need me.'

Five

THE MOON WAS rising behind the elephant apple trees on the opposite bank of the lake, there was a dense shadow on the water. On this side, the tender leaves of the butterfly tree were red like the eyes of a child just awoken, its flowers the colour of pure gold, a strong fragrance hung heavily like a pall, like a fog of perfume as it were. Fireflies glittered on the branches of the Queen's Flower tree. On the paved steps leading into the water, silent like a stone, sat Sarala. There was no breeze, no trembling of leaves, the water was like a polished silver mirror framed in black shadow.

'May I?' came the question from somewhere behind her.

'Of course,' answered Sarala graciously. Ramen took his seat on the stairs, near her feet. 'What kind of a spot is that, Ramen-dada?' said Sarala fretfully. 'Come up now.'

'Do you know that all descriptions of goddesses begin with their feet? If there's room by your side I'll take it later,' replied Ramen. 'Give me your hand, let me begin the welcome in Western style.'

Taking Sarala's hand, he kissed it. 'Greetings from the empress,' he said.

Rising to his feet, he put a streak of aabir, the coloured powder of Holi, on her forehead.

'What's all this?'

'Don't you know it's the full moon of Holi? There's a burst of colours on your plants, your branches. Spring touches not the body but the heart with colour. But that colour must be visible to the eye, or else, O forest goddess, you shall remain in exile here in this glade.'

'I can never match you for words.'

'Who needs words? It's the male birds that sing, the females only need to listen in silence. Now let me sit by your side.'

He did. Both of them were silent for some while. Suddenly Sarala said, 'I need your advice on how to go to jail, Ramenda.'

'There are so many ways to go to jail, and it's so easy now that it's far more difficult to offer advice on how not to go to jail. The British policeman's whistle simply won't allow us to cower in fear at home.'

'No, I'm not joking, I'm convinced that's my only escape.'

'Tell me properly what's on your mind.'

'I will. But you have to see Adit-da to understand.'

'I've noticed signs.'

'I was alone in the verandah this afternoon, leafing through a catalogue of pictures of flowering plants that's just come from America; Adit-da usually starts me off in the garden after his tea every day at four-thirty. But today he just wandered around absent-mindedly, not even glancing at the gardeners as they worked. I thought he would come up to me in the verandah but he hesitated and went back. Such a tall, strapping man, always rushing about, always working hard; so very alert, a stern taskmaster but ever ready with a forgiving smile; imagine such a man losing his pace, paying no attention to anything, lost somewhere in the depths of his thoughts.

He eventually came up to me with slow footsteps. Any other day he would have pointed at his watch and said "It's time", I would have joined him at once. Instead he drew up a stool by me and sat down heavily. "Looking at the catalogue?" he said. Taking it from me, he started leafing through it. But he didn't seem to be reading. Suddenly he glanced at me, as though he had finally decided to say something to me. Then

171

instantly he lowered his eyes to the catalogue again, saying, "Have you seen, Shori, how large the nasturtiums are?" He sounded completely exhausted. Then he didn't speak again for a long time, just kept turning the pages. He looked at me again, then slammed the book shut and rose, dropping it in my lap. "Aren't we going to the garden?" I asked. "No, I have to go out, it's important," he said, and left as if tearing himself away.'

'What did Adit-da want to tell you? What do you think?'

'He had come to say, one of your gardens has been destroyed already, now an order has been issued to destroy the other one, too.'

'If that does happen, Shori, I won't be able to go to jail.'

'How can I stop you?' said Sarala with a wan smile. 'The king emperor himself will clear the way.'

'How can I march off to jail, while everybody stops and stares at my clanking chains, while you languish in the street like a flower plucked off its stem? In that case I'll have to reform at this ripe old age.'

'What will you do, then?'

'I'll declare war on your unlucky planets. Drive them out of your future. And then go on my long holiday—why, it could even be to the Andaman jail.'

'I cannot hide anything at all from you. It's becoming clearer to me by the day. And I'm going to tell you what it is, if you don't mind.'

'I will if you don't tell me.'

'I've grown up with Adit-da—not like brother and sister, but like two brothers. We dug in the garden, working side by side, trimming the plants. I was six when my mother and aunt died of typhoid within a couple of days of each other. My father died two years later. My uncle—his elder brother—had hoped from the bottom of his heart that I would protect his garden with my life. He groomed me for just that purpose. He couldn't stop himself from trusting people. He hadn't doubted for a moment that the friends he had lent money to would repay him so that he could free the garden of the debts he had run up for it. Adit-da was the only one to repay him—no one else did. You may know some of this history but I feel the urge today to tell it all over again.'

'It all seems new to me.'

'After that, you know, the whole enterprise sank. When it was rescued from the floods and hauled up to dry land, I discovered my fate was moored to Adit-da's. We came together as before—like brothers, like friends. Since then, just as it's true that Adit-da has been my saviour, it's equally true that I have been his. As far as I'm concerned, nothing has changed. I have no reason whatsoever to hold back. I went back to being the same age I was, to the same relationship, when we were together. We could have gone on this way forever. There's nothing more to say.'

'Finish what you were saying.'

'Why did I suddenly have to be rudely reminded of my age? The illusion of the past, when we did things together, was destroyed in a single moment. I'm sure you know everything, Ramen-da, nothing escapes your eye. Boudi's anger surprised me at first, I didn't understand it. I hadn't scrutinized myself all this time, but when I saw myself by the fire of boudidi's displeasure, I had to confess to myself. Do you understand what I'm saying?'

'A love that you had buried when you were young is flowering again.'

'What can I do now? How do I run away from myself?' she said, clasping Ramen's hands.

Ramen was silent.

'The longer I stay here, the more I wrong people.'

'Wrong whom?'

'Wrong boudi.'

173

'Look, Sarala, I don't go by textbook theory. What is the truth that you will apply to rule between conflicting claims? The two of you have been together so long—where was boudi then?'

'What are you saying, Ramen-da! What kind of unfair justification is this of one's wishes. We have to think of Adit-da too.'

'Of course we do. Do you suppose the blow that felled you didn't make an impact on him too?'

'Ramen? Is that you?' came a voice from behind them.

'Yes, dada.' Ramen rose.

'Your boudi has sent for you, the ayah came to tell me.'

Ramen left, Sarala made to leave, too.

'Don't go, Shori, stay a while,' said Aditya. When she saw his expression, Sarala felt her heart was about to break. The noble soul, normally so absorbed in his work that he forgot himself, seemed to be tossed about like a rudderless ship on the high seas.

'We began our lives as one in this world,' said Aditya. 'Our bond is so natural that it's impossible to even imagine anything breaking it. Isn't that so, Shori?'

'There's no choice but to accept that what's one in the seed always splits when it grows, Aditya-da.'

'But that split is only visible outside for the benefit of the eyes only. The souls stay joined. Today we're under attack to be separated. I could never have imagined it would hurt so much. Do you know that we're under attack suddenly, shori?'

'I do, my dear. I knew even before you did.'

'Can you bear it, Shori?'

'I have to.'

'Can women bear more pain than us, I wonder?'

'You men fight unhappiness, but generations of women have only borne unhappiness. They have nothing to bank on besides their tears and their endurance.'

174

'I will not let them tear you away from me, I will not. It's wrong, it's cruel.' He screwed up his fists to battle an invisible enemy in the sky.

Taking Aditya's hand from his lap on to her own, Sarala traced her fingertips over it. She spoke, almost to herself, 'It's not a matter of right or wrong, my dear; when the ties of a relationship become a noose, it's not just a single person who feels it tighten around his throat; everyone starts tugging at it, whom can you blame?'

'I know you'll be able to bear it. I remember that day—what lovely hair you had then, you still do. You were asleep after lunch, your hair spread out over your pillow, I went and cut at least six inches with a pair of scissors. You awoke immediately, stood up, your black eyes looking an even deeper black. "You think you can get the better of me?" you said, and, snatching the scissors from my hand, you cut what was left of your long hair. Your uncle was astonished at the sight. "What's all this?" he asked. "Long hair makes me hot," you answered, nonchalantly. He didn't ask questions, didn't rebuke you, only took the scissors to crop your hair evenly all round. Your uncle, after all!'

'How clever of you,' Sarala said smiling. 'You think I forgave you? Far from it. It was I who got the better of you that day, not the other way round. Am I right?'

'Absolutely right. I was all but in tears at the sight of that shorn head. I couldn't come near you the next day. I was so embarrassed, I skulked in the study. You came in and dragged me off to the garden, as though nothing had happened. There was this other time, an unseasonal spring storm had blown the roof off the room where I slept, you came and...'

'No more, Adit-da,' she sighed. 'Those days won't come back,' she said, preparing to leave.

Aditya clung to her hand desperately. 'No, don't go, not just yet, it *will* be time to go some day but now...'

175

As he spoke, he became agitated. 'But why do you have to go at all, ever? What wrong have we done? Is this a test for ten years of married life? What's all the jealousy for! In that case I have to wipe off twenty-three years of history, from the time I first met you.'

'I cannot speak for all the twenty-three years, my dear, but has there really been no cause for jealousy in these last few moments of those twenty-three years? The truth must be told—why fool ourselves? Nothing must be unclear between you and me.'

Aditya sat mutely. Then he said, 'It isn't unclear any more. Deep within me I have realized my world is nothing without you. Nobody but he who gave you to me in the first light of my life can snatch you away from me.'

'Don't say all this, Adit-da, don't make it worse. Allow me to think it over calmly.'

'Thinking it over will not undo things. When we started our lives together, protected by our uncle, it wasn't after thinking things over. Is there a shovel on this planet that can dig those days out of the earth? I cannot speak for you, Shori, but I don't have the power to do it.'

'Don't weaken me, I beg of you. Don't make my escape harder.'

Clasping both her hands with his, Aditya said, 'There won't be any escape, I won't let you. I am in love with you, and my heart is overflowing tonight because I am able to tell you this so naturally, so simply. What lay concealed in the bud for twenty-three years is blooming today—perhaps it is divine providence. I can tell you that denying it will be cowardice, immoral.

'Shhh, no more. Excuse me just for this night, excuse me.'

'I'm the one who seeks your compassion, Shori, I'm the one who must keep asking your forgiveness till the end of my life.

176

Why was I so blind? Why did I not see you, why did I have to make the mistake of getting married? You didn't, I know just how many prospective grooms came seeking your hand.'

'Jyathamashai had dedicated me to his garden, you see, otherwise perhaps…'

'No—the truth shone brightly in the depth of your heart. You had committed yourself to it, unknowingly. Why didn't you alert me? Why did our paths have to diverge?'

'Let it be. When you have to accept something, whom can you argue with in refusal? What use is it to chafe? We can find an answer tomorrow morning.'

'All right, I won't say anything else. But I will leave something with you that will speak for me, on this moonlit night.'

When he worked in the garden, Aditya always had a pouch at his waist to hold whatever he collected. From it he took a small bunch of rose-coloured chestnut flowers. 'I know you love the chestnut flower. Can I drape them over your shoulder? I brought a safety pin, see.'

Sarala didn't protest. Aditya put the flowers in place, taking his time. Sarala rose to her feet, Aditya stood opposite her, gazing at her the way the moon was gazing down from the sky. 'You amaze me, Shori, you amaze me,' he said.

Snatching her hand back, Sarala ran away. Instead of following her, Aditya watched her in silence as long as she was visible. Then, he sat down on the steps that lead into the water.

'Dinner is served,' a servant arrived to announce.

'I don't want any,' said Aditya.

Six

'You sent for me, boudi?' asked Ramen, from the door. 'Come in,' said Neeraja, clearing her choked throat.

All the lights in the room were out. The window was open, the moonlight shone on the bed, on Neeraja's face and on the laburnums Aditya had given her. She was propped up against her pillows, gazing out at the garden. A row of areca trees was visible beyond the orchid room. A breeze had just sprung up, the leaves had begun to sway, the fragrance of mangoes was in the air. The sound of drums and singing could be heard in the distance, Holi was in full swing in the slums where the bullock cart drivers lived. On a plate on the floor were arranged a few Indian sweets and some aabir—gifts from the doorman. All the house was silent today lest the patient's rest be disturbed. From the trees outside came the unending repartee between a pair of brainfever birds, neither willing to admit defeat.

Ramen drew a stool up to Neeraja's bedside. Neeraja didn't speak for a long time, afraid she would break down in tears if she tried. Her lips trembled, pain coiled up within her. She controlled herself after a while, crushing the petals shed by the laburnums in her fist. Then, without a word, she handed a letter to Ramen. It was written by Aditya. It said:

> After so many years together, I suddenly saw it was possible for you to doubt my devotion. I feel embarrassed to have to argue this out with you. Given your current frame of mind, anything I do or say will have a contrary effect.

This unnecessary torment will hurt your already weak health every moment. It's better for me to stay away until you're calmer. I also realize that you want me to dismiss Sarala from this house, from her work. Perhaps I'll have to. I've realized after much thought there's no other way. Still I must tell you that all my education, my learning, my achievements are thanks to meshomashai. He was the one who showed me the path to fulfilment. Today Sarala, the apple of his eye, is penniless and helpless. It would be immoral to set her adrift; I cannot do it even to honour my love for you.

After considerable thought, I've decided to start a new division in our business, for growing flower and vegetable seeds. A house with a garden in Maniktala is available; I'm going to settle Sarala there, in charge of that division. I don't have enough money to start this project, so I'll have to pawn this house of ours to raise the money. Don't forget, Sarala's uncle lent me the capital to build this garden without charging any interest—I heard he actually had to borrow some of the money he gave me. Not just that, he also gave me plants, seeds of some very rare flowers, orchids, lawnmowers, and other equipment completely free of cost so that I could get the business going. If he hadn't created this wonderful opportunity for me, I would have been a thirty-rupees-a-month clerk; I wouldn't have had the chance to marry you either.

After my conversation with you the one question that's been confronting me repeatedly is this: was it I who offered a home to Sarala or was it she who offered one to me? I had forgotten this simple truth, it was you who reminded me. Now you must remember it too. Don't imagine for a moment Sarala is dependent on me. I'll never be able to repay my debt to her and her uncle, nor will there ever be a limit to her claim on me. I will keep in mind that I must try

179

to ensure you never have to meet her. But today I realized like never before that my relationship with her is not one that can be severed. I'm not able to tell you all, I am too overcome with sorrow. If you can surmise the truth, well and good, otherwise, for the first time in my life, my agony will remain unexpressed to you.

Ramen read the letter through twice. Then he fell silent.

'Say something,' said Neeraja, in despair.

Still, Ramen didn't respond.

Then Neeraja flung herself on her bed, beating her head on her pillow, saying, 'What I have done is terrible, terrible. But can't any of you understand what it was that drove me mad?'

'What are you doing, boudi? Calm down, you will collapse.'

'It's this body that's brought me to such a pass, what do I care for it? "I don't trust him"? Where did that come from? This is nothing but my lack of trust in myself, with this invalid body of mine. Where is that Neeru of his today, she whom he would call Malini, his girl of the garlands, whom he would call Bonolokkhi, his goddess of the woods! Who has taken her glade away? I didn't have just the one name, you know. When he worked late into the night, and I stayed up waiting to serve him his dinner, he called me Annapurna—his provider of sustenance. In the evenings, when he rested on the steps leading into the lake, when I used to serve him his paan on a bed of jasmine on a silver plate, he would smile and call me Tambulkarankabahini—the carrier of his spice. He would take my advice on every aspect of running the household. Why, he even used to call me the Home Secretary. I was like the swollen river flowing to meet sea, spreading myself through a hundred different streams; but now all those streams have dried up overnight, you can see the rocks at the bottom.'

'You'll get better, boudi, you'll take possession of your throne again in all your glory.'

'Don't give me false hope, thakurpo. I can hear what the doctors say. That's why I'm like a hopeless beggar, trying to cling so desperately to my world of happiness.'

'Why do you have to do that, boudi? You have given all of yourself to your home and your husband. Can anything be a greater truth? And you got as much as you gave, which woman can claim to have got quite as much? If the doctors are indeed right, if it is indeed time to leave, then give it up as nobly as you received it in the first place. Why should the glory in which you have spent all these years be diminished as you depart? When you leave, let everyone remember your nobility.'

'My heart breaks, thakurpo, my heart breaks. I could easily have left behind all my happy years and gone with a smile. But will there not be lit even a single lamp to mourn me, in some small corner of the house? The very thought makes me not want to die. Has God ruled that Sarala will seize it all, completely?'

'I'm going to be truthful, boudi, don't be angry. I don't understand you at all. Can't you happily bequeath what you can no longer enjoy yourself on someone whom you've given so much already all these years? Must your love have such a black mark hanging over it forever? You're about to demolish with your own hands, the respect you commanded in your own home. You will escape the pain, but it will hurt us always. I'm pleading with you not to reduce your lifelong generosity into pettyness in these final moments.'

Neeraja began to sob. Ramen sat in silence, making no attempt to console her. When her sobs abated Neeraja sat up on her bed. 'I have something to ask of you, thakurpo.'

'Just give the order, boudi.'

'Let me tell you, when my tears flood my heart I look at that picture of Ramakrishna. But his sayings do not reach my soul. I'm a small, mean-spirited person. Show me the way to him—you have to, somehow or other. Or else I won't be able to sever my ties and attachments. The very house where I led a happy life will be haunted till eternity by my tears of sorrow, after I die; deliver me from that fate, deliver me, I beg of you.'

'You know very well, boudi, that I'm what they call a heathen in the scriptures. I don't follow any rules. Prabhash Mitra insisted on taking me to meet his spiritual guru—I escaped before I could be tied down. Even jail sentences are for a fixed time, this imprisonment stretches beyond time.'

'You're strong, thakurpo, you will never understand the threat that hangs over me. I can see clearly that the more I thrash about, the deeper I sink into the water. I'm not able to prevent it.'

'Let me tell you something, boudi. You're going to burn with jealousy as long as you think your treasures are being snatched away. You will never find peace. But calm yourself and say, just once— "I'm giving it away. I'm giving away what is most priceless of all to the person I love the most." Your burden will be relieved in an instant. Your heart will be filled with joy. You won't need a saviour. Say it now— "Here, now I give it away, I'm not holding on to anything, I'm giving away all I had, I'm liberated, prepared for purification, I won't bind anyone with even a thread of unhappiness."'

'Oh thakurpo, tell me, tell me again and again. Whatever I have been able to give him all this while has been enough to bring me joy, what I cannot give today is what hurts so much. I'll give it away, I'll give it away, I'll give away all I have—not later, now. Go fetch him for me.'

'Not tonight, boudi, build your resolve over the next few days, let it be easy to do what you have determined to.'

'No, I cannot take it any more. Ever since he said he would leave this house and live in the Japanese room, my bed has become a funeral pyre. If he doesn't return the night won't pass, I shall die of heartbreak. Call Sarala too, I will pluck out the needle lodged in my heart, I will not be afraid—I give you my word.'

'It's not time yet, boudi, not tonight.'

'My fear is that my time will be done. Fetch them this instant.' Looking at the picture of Paramhansa, she joined her hands in prayer. 'Give me strength, my lord, give me strength, free this foolish, despicable woman. My unhappiness has kept my god at bay, all my prayers, my worship, have dried up. I want to say something, thakurpo, please don't turn me down.'

'What is it? Tell me.'

'Let me visit my prayer room for ten minutes please, it will give me strength, I won't be afraid any more.'

'All right, go, I won't stop you.'

'Ayah!'

'Yes, khnokhi.'

'Help me to the prayer room.'

'What! But the doctor...'

'The doctor can't keep death away, do you suppose he can keep my gods away?'

'Take her, ayah, it won't do any harm, actually it will be good for her.'

After Neeraja had left, leaning on the ayah for support, Aditya entered.

'Where's Neeru? Why isn't she in the room?'

'She'll be back any minute, she's gone to her prayer room.'

'Prayer room! But it isn't close by. The doctor's forbidden it.'

'Don't listen to the doctor, dada. This will work better than his medicines. All she'll do is put some flowers there, say her prayers, and come back.'

When he had sent his letter to her, Aditya hadn't known that the script which fate had written for him—in invisible ink—was suddenly going to become clear under the heat applied to it. He had originally meant to tell Sarala, 'There's no way out, separation is inevitable.' But when it was time, he had ended up saying just the opposite. Then, sitting on those same steps, by moonlight, he had told himself again and again that he may have discovered the truth late in life, but he couldn't repudiate it just for that reason. He had done no wrong, nothing to be ashamed of. What would be wrong would be to conceal the truth. He would not conceal it, he was determined; let the outcome be what it may. Aditya had realized, quite clearly, that if he were to allow Sarala to be excised from the centre of his life, from the centre of his work, the loneliness, the void would destroy everything, even his work.

'I know that you know all about us, Ramen.'

'Yes, I do.'

'I'm going to end it all today, reveal everything.'

'You're not the only one involved, dada. It's not just a matter of ridding yourself of your burden; there's boudi, too, to be considered. The bonds of family are more complex than you think.'

'I will not be able to maintain a lie between your sister-in-law and me. You do accept that there is nothing wrong in my relationship with Sarala since childhood?'

'Of course I do.'

'I had not realized there was a deep love hidden beneath that simple relationship—is that our fault?'

'Who says it is?'

'If today I were to conceal it, I would be guilty of lying. I'm going to say it with my head held high.'

'Why would you conceal it—and why would you announce it ceremoniously either? Boudi has found out, on her own, what there is to know. The knot of her misery will unravel on its own very soon; don't pull at it unnecessarily. Listen to what she wants to tell you; the response will be obvious to you.'

Seeing Neeraja return, Ramen left.

Upon entering the room, at the sight of Aditya, Neeraja flung herself on the floor at his feet, declaring in a voice choked with tears, 'Forgive me, forgive me, I have wronged you. Don't forsake me after all this time, don't cast me aside.'

Taking her hands and pulling her to her feet, Aditya folded her to his breast and led her to her bed, gently easing her on to it.

'I cannot understand your pain, Neeru,' he said. Neeraja's tears continued, unabated. Aditya ran his fingertips lightly over her forehead. Clasping Aditya's hands and pressing it to her breast, Neeraja said, 'Tell me truly that you forgive me. Unless you're content I will not be happy even after I die.'

'You know very well, Neeru, we have had differences of opinion from time to time, but has the bond between our hearts ever been broken because of that?'

'You never left home earlier. Why then, this time? What has made you behave so cruelly?'

'It was wrong of me, Neeru, you have to forgive me.'

'What *are* you saying! *You* are the only one who can punish me, who can reward me. I was in this state because I tried to judge you in a fit of indignation... I had asked thakurpo to fetch Sarala, why isn't she here yet?'

The mention of Sarala was a sharp blow to Aditya's heart. He hoped this problem could be set aside for at least the day. 'Not now, it's late.'

'There, I think they're waiting outside the door. Come in both of you. Come, thakurpo.'

Ramen entered with Sarala. Leaving her bed, Neeraja rose to her feet. Sarala bent to touch her feet with her hand. 'Come here, my sister, come to me.'

Taking Sarala's hand, Neeraja made her sit on the bed. Pulling her jewellery case out from under her pillow and taking out a pearl necklace, she put it round Sarala's neck.

'Once I had wished for this necklace to be around my neck when my body was burnt on the pyre,' she said. 'But this is better. You must wear this necklace all your life. Your cousin knows how often I've put this necklace on to mark special occasions. He will remember those occasions if you keep the necklace on.'

'I'm unworthy, didi, unworthy, why must you shame me?'

Neeraja had thought of this as part of her great renunciation. But she didn't realize that the jealousy that burnt deep within her showed itself through this gesture.

Aditya sensed how much the whole thing had hurt Sarala. 'Why don't you give me that necklace, Sarala? It's not as valuable to anyone else as it is to me. I cannot part with it for anyone else.'

'That's my fate,' said Neeraja. 'No matter what I say, no one understands. I was told that it had been proposed that you should leave this garden and go elsewhere. I will never let that happen. I will keep you involved with every aspect of my home, this necklace is a symbol of that vow; that I have transferred my bond to you so that I can die in peace.'

'You're making a mistake, didi, don't try to bind me, it will come to no good.'

'What do you mean?'

'I won't say anything but the truth. You could have trusted me all this while but you do not trust me any more. I'm saying this openly, in everyone's presence. I am not going to deprive anyone of the chance to seize what fate deprived me of. Here is my tribute to you: I am going now. The fault is not mine, the fault is that god's whom I had naïvely trusted and worshipped day and night. All that is over now.'

Sarala left the room with quick steps. Unable to restrain himself, Aditya followed her.

'Thakurpo, what have I done, thakurpo? Tell me, say something.'

'That's why I told you not to talk to her tonight.'

'But why? I have given up everything with an open heart. Didn't she even understand?'

'Of course she did. She understood your heart isn't open at all. You spoke with a false note.'

'My heart refuses to be cleansed. Even after so many blows. Who will cleanse it? Save me, my Lord. Whom can I call my own, thakurpo, whom can I turn to?'

'I'm here, boudi. I will look after you. Go to sleep now.'

'How will I go to sleep. If he leaves home again I will not be able to sleep unless I die.'

'He cannot leave. He has neither the wish nor the strength to do it. Here are your sleeping pills, I'm not leaving till I see you sleep.'

'Go, thakurpo, see where they've gone, else I'll go myself, I don't care if I collapse.'

'Very well, I'm going.'

Seven

'Why did you come?' said Sarala when she saw Aditya following her. 'It wasn't right of you. Go back. I will not let you get involved with me this way.'

'It's irrelevant whether you will or will not, I'm involved already. Good or bad—the outcome is not in our control.'

'We can talk about that later, go back now and calm the patient down.'

'The discussion about the new division of our business…'

'Not today. Give me a few days to think things over, I do not have the strength now to think.'

Ramen appeared, saying, 'Go along, dada, give boudi her sleeping pills and help her sleep, don't delay now. You mustn't let her talk at all. It's very late.'

'Isn't there a meeting at Sraddhananda park tomorrow?' said Sarala, after Aditya had left.

'There is.'

'Aren't you going?'

'I'd meant to. But I won't be able to this time.'

'Why not?'

'What use is it explaining that to you?'

'People will condemn you as a coward.'

'Those who do not like me certainly will.'

'Then listen to me, and I shall rescue you. You *have* to go to the meeting.'

'Explain clearly.'

'I will go to the meeting too, flag in hand.'

'I see.'

'I can accept the police stopping me, but not you.'

'All right, I shan't.'

'Is that a promise?'

'A promise.'

'We'll go together at five in the evening tomorrow.'

'We will, but the devils won't let us be together after that.'

As they were conversing, Aditya arrived. 'Why did you come away so soon?' asked Sarala.

'Neeraja was so exhausted by a few words that she fell asleep. I stole away.'

'I'm going now, I have things to do,' said Ramen.

'Don't forget to find a house for me,' said Sarala with a smile.

'Don't worry. I know just the place,' he said and left.

Eight

SARALA WAS SEATED. She rose to her feet, saying, 'Don't tell me the things that are not to be said tonight, I beg of you.'

'Don't worry, I won't say a word.'

'All right then, I want to say something. Promise to keep my request.'

'Unless it's impossible to keep, you know I will.'

'There's no doubt that it won't do for me to stay here. I would have been happy to have looked after didi at this time, but I'm not fortunate enough for that privilege. I have no choice but to go away. Wait, let me finish. You've heard the doctor say she doesn't have long to go. The thorn sticking in her heart must be plucked out before that. Don't let my shadow fall on her life during this time.'

'But what if my heart casts a shadow on its own?'

'Don't speak of yourself so disdainfully. Yours is not the soft, wet soil of the hearts and minds of other Bengali young men. Never, I know you.'

'Take this vow for me,' she said, taking Aditya's hands. 'Fulfil the last days of didi's life generously. Make her forget that I shattered her happiness with my presence.'

Aditya stood in silence.

'Promise me, my dear.'

'I will, but so must you keep a request of mine. Promise me you will.'

'The difference between you and me is that if I make you promise something it's possible, but what you will make me promise may turn out to be impossible.'

'No, it will not.'

'All right, tell me.'

'There's nothing wrong in telling you what I tell myself all the time. I will do as you say, and it will be possible for me to do it if I know with certainty that one day you will fulfil all my emptiness. Why don't you say something?'

'I don't know, my dear, what obstacles may come in the way of fulfilling that promise.'

'Is there an obstacle within you? Tell me that first.'

'Why do you break my heart? Don't you know there are things whose light goes out when they are said in words?'

'All right, I have heard enough, and with that I will do my duty.'

'You won't look back any more now?'

'No, but I wish I could put a stamp of an unsaid promise on your face.'

'Don't force what is simple. Never mind now.'

'All right, then let me ask—what will you do now, where will you live?'

'Ramen-da has taken the responsibility.'

'Ramen give you shelter and support! What means does that vagabond have of his own?'

'Don't worry. It's a secure shelter. Not his own property, but nothing will come in the way.'

'You'll tell me, won't you?'

'Of course I will, I promise; but you must make sure not to fret, for even a moment, to want to see me.'

'Will your heart not fret either?'

'If it does nobody but the Almighty shall know.'

'Very well. But will you leave the beggar's bowl empty before you go?'

His eyes misted over.

Sarala came closer and raised her face.

Nine

'Roshni.'

'Yes, khnokhi.'

'Why isn't Sarala to be seen anywhere?'

'What do you mean, don't you know? The government has sent her to jail.'

'Why, what did she do?'

'She conspired with the watchman and entered the chamber of the governor general's wife.'

'Whatever for?'

'To steal the casket with the seal of the empress, such was her audacity.'

'What would she gain from it?'

'What do you mean! That seal is all-powerful. She could have had the governor general hanged. It's the seal that runs the kingdom.'

'And thakurpo?'

'They found a burglar's rod in his turban. He's been sent to another jail, rigorous imprisonment for fifty years. I want to ask you something, khnokhi, before she left Sarala-didi gave me her expensive saffron sari. "For your daughter-in-law," she told me. It made me cry. I had made her life miserable. The government won't arrest me if I keep the sari, will they?'

'Don't worry. But go quickly and fetch me the newspaper from the drawing room.'

Neeraja read the newspaper and was amazed Aditya hadn't informed her of such a development. Was this out of contempt? The girl has gone to jail and won. As if I couldn't have gone to jail too if I'd been strong enough. I could have smiled all the way to the gallows.

'Have you seen what your Sarala-didi has done, Roshni? To behave like this in the presence of thousands of people, a girl from a decent family too...'

'It terrifies me when I think of it. Robbers and thieves are nothing compared to her. Shame on her!'

'She has this streak of foolhardiness. Always going to extremes, from the garden to the prison. Even in her final hours she won't forsake her pride.'

The ayah was reminded of the saffron sari. 'But she has a generous heart, khnokhi,' she said.

Neeraja felt a jolt. She said, as though waking up suddenly, 'You're right, Roshni, you're right. I'd forgotten. When you're ill you always feel miserable. I've become so mean. Shame on me, I want to slap myself. Fetch Ganesh at once.'

When the ayah left she sat down with a pencil to write a letter. Ganesh arrived. 'Can you take this letter to Sarala-didi at the jail?'

Ganesh was proud of his abilities. 'I can. It'll need some money. But what have you written, ma, for the letter will go through the police.'

'I admire your generosity,' Neeraja read out. 'When you're out of jail, you'll see that my path has converged with yours.'

'That business about the path doesn't sound innocent. Let me show it to our lawyer before sending it.'

Ganesh left. Paying a silent tribute to Ramen, Neeraja said, 'You're my saviour, thakurpo.'

193

Ten

ADITYA CAME IN with some medicine in a cup.

'What's all this?' said Neeraja.

'The doctor has asked for the medicine to be taken every hour.'

'So you couldn't find anyone else in the neighbourhood to bring it to me? If you're so anxious, why don't you also add a nurse for the daytime?'

'If I can use the pretext of taking care of you to come to you, why should I let the opportunity pass?'

'I'd be far happier if you worked in the garden on some pretext. While I lie here, the garden is rotting every day.'

'Let it. Once you get better, we'll work on it together, just like before.'

'With Sarala gone, you're all by yourself, which is why you can't concentrate on your work. But what else can you do? Don't let the garden run up losses.'

'I'm not thinking of losses, Neeru. It was you who had ensured I never thought of the garden as my business enterprise; that's why work was a joy. My heart isn't in it any more.'

'Why are you so disheartened? You were working diligently even a few days ago. Don't be so upset if something goes wrong for a few days.'

'Shall I switch the fan on?'

'Don't concern yourself with all this—it isn't your line of work. It just makes me more agitated. If you're looking for a way to pass the time, you have your Horticulturists' Club, don't you?'

'I looked all over the garden for the lilies you love, couldn't find a single one. The plants aren't strong this year because it didn't rain very well.'

'What nonsense. Fetch Hala instead, I'll manage the garden from my bed. Are you telling me that my garden should be on a sickbed just because I am? Listen to me now. Have the dry season flower plants removed and re-lay the soil. There are sacks of mustard husks in the room beneath the stairs. Hala has the key.'

'Really! Hala didn't say anything.'

'Why would he? You people have harassed him so much. Just like the raw young manager who ignores the veteran clerk.'

'If I were to tell the truth about Hala, you wouldn't like it.'

'All right, I'll direct him from my bed, you'll see if the garden isn't transformed in a couple of days. Bring the map of the garden to me, and my garden diary. I'll mark everything out on the map with a pencil and make the arrangements.'

'I'm not going to be involved at all?'

'No. I will stamp my mark on the garden before I go. I won't keep any of those bottle palms by the side of the road, I'm warning you; I'm going to plant a row of casuarina trees there. Don't shake our head, you'll see when I am finished. I'm not keeping that lawn you've made; I'll have a marble platform instead.'

'Will a platform fit in? It's a little...what you might call nouveau riche.'

'Oh, keep quiet. It will fit in perfectly. You can't say no. For the next few days this garden is going to be mine, mine alone. Then I will gift this garden of mine to you. You must have thought I have no strength left—I'll show you what I can do. I need three more gardeners, and about six labourers.

I remember you saying once that I had not learnt yet how to make a garden beautiful. I'm going to test myself now to find out whether I have. You have to remember that it's my garden, mine alone, I shall never give up my rights to it.'

'Very well then, I shall have nothing to do with it.'

'You can keep yourself busy with your shop. There's plenty of work there, after all.'

'So I'm forbidden to be with you too?'

'Yes, I'm no longer someone you can be with all the time. I can at best remind you of someone else, how will that help.'

'Very well, then. I'll come to you only when you can tolerate me. Send for me. I brought gardenias for you today in the tray, I'll leave them on your bed, if you don't mind,' said Aditya and rose.

'No, don't go away, stay a while,' said Neeraja, taking his hand. Pointing to a flower in the vase, she said, 'Do you know what that's called?'

Knowing the answer that would please her, Aditya lied. 'No, I don't.'

'I do. Shall I tell you? Petunia. You think I know nothing, that I'm ignorant.'

'You're my fellow-traveller, if you're ignorant, you're at least as ignorant as I am. We're equal partners in the business of ignorance in our lives.'

'That business is winding to a close for me. That doorman there who's slicing his tobacco, even he will still be there in the gatehouse—but very soon now, I won't. That bullock cart which has tipped out its load of rocky coal pieces and is now on its way back, its trips will continue, but my heart won't go on beating.' Suddenly clutching Aditya's hand, she said, 'Will I not be here at all? Will nothing of me remain? Tell me, you've read so much, tell me truly.'

'I know as much as the people who wrote those books. I've only travelled close to death's door, not entered it.'

'Tell me please, will nothing of me remain? Nothing at all?'

'If you can be here now, you will be here then too.'

'Of course I will, it can never happen that the garden will be there and I won't. The crows will return home in the fading light of dusk just as they do now, the branches of the nut trees will sway before my eyes just as they do now. When that happens, remember—I am here, I am here, I am here all over the garden. Imagine that when your hair blows in the wind, my fingers are running through it. Tell me, will you remember?'

'Yes, I'll remember,' Aditya was forced to say, though not convincingly.

'Those writers of yours who write those books, they're not wise at all, they know nothing. I'm sure I do, trust me; I'll remain, I'll remain right here, I'll remain with all of you, I can see it all so clearly. I'm telling you now, I give you my word, I'll look after all the flowers and plants and trees in your garden, even better than I used to earlier. I won't need anyone's help, anyone at all.'

Neeraja had been lying down on her bed; now she sat up, saying, 'Be kind to me afterwards, be kind to me. Always remember I loved you so. Give me a place the same way you have given me a place in your home, with just as much love. In your mind, give me the flowers of the season just as you do now. If you're cruel, I'll never be able to stay here. If you take away my garden, I will have to wander about in emptiness.' Tears streamed from her eyes.

Rising from the stool, Aditya sat on the bed. Drawing Neerja's head to his breast, he caressed it softly. 'Don't, Neeru, it will make you worse,' he said.

'Forget all that. I don't want anything else, all I want is you— with everything I have. I want to tell you something—don't be angry with me, don't be angry,' she said in a choked voice.

After she had calmed down a little, she said, 'I've been unfair to Sarala. I promise you I won't be like that any more.

Forgive me for what has happened. But love me, love me please, I'll do all that you want me to.'

'Your heart was as ill as your body, Neeru, that's why you tortured yourself so much.'

'Let me tell you. Since last night, I have been swearing to myself that the next time I see her I will draw her to me without rancour, like I would a sister. Help me keep this final vow of mine. Tell me I will not be deprived of your love, that I will be able to share my love with everyone before I go.'

Without answering, Aditya kissed her face, her forehead repeatedly. Neeraja's eyes closed. A little later she said, 'I'm counting the days to Sarala's release. What if I die before that? What if I cannot tell her before I go that my heart is cleansed? Turn on the lamp now. Read Akshay Baral's *Esha* to me.' She pulled the book out from beneath her pillow. Aditya read to her.

Just as she was nodding off listening to Aditya read, the ayah entered. 'Letter!' she announced. The spell broke, jolting Neeraja into wakefulness. Her heart began to beat heavily. A friend had informed Aditya that the jail was running out of space; among the prisoners who were to be released early was Sarala.

Aditya's heart leapt, he suppressed his elation.

'Who's it from, what does it say?' asked Neeraja.

Lest his voice shake as he read it, Aditya handed the letter to Neeraja. She looked at him. He was silent but speech wasn't necessary; Neeraja couldn't utter a word for some time either. Then she said, rather loudly, 'Then there's not much time. She'll be here today. You must bring her to me.'

'What is it? What's the matter! Neeru! Nurse, is the doctor here?'

'Yes, in the drawing room.'

'Fetch him immediately. Ah, doctor! She was fine just a moment ago, speaking normally and suddenly she fell unconscious.'

The doctor was grave as he examined his patient's pulse.

A little later, Neeraja opened her eyes and said at once, 'You *have* to save my life, doctor. I cannot go without seeing Sarala, that won't be right. I must give her my blessing—my final blessing.'

Her eyes were about to close again, her grip grew tighter. 'I will keep my word, thakurpo,' she said, 'I shall not die like a miser.'

Her consciousness grew dim, all became indistinct—then like a dying lamp the flame of her life blazed again. 'When will Sarala come?' she kept asking her husband.

'Roshni!' she called out from time to time.

'Yes, khnokhi,' the ayah said.

'Fetch thakurpo this instant.' Once, she muttered to herself, 'What's going to become of me, thakurpo? I will give everything, I will, I will, everything, I will give everything.'

It was nine o'clock at night. A candle burnt faintly in a corner of Neeraja's room. The fragrance of magnolia hung in the air. An inky cluster of trees was visible through the open window, and above them the Orion constellation in the sky. Aditya left Sarala at the door, thinking that the patient might be asleep, and approached Neeraja's bed gently.

He saw her lips moving; as though she were muttering an incantation soundlessly. She seemed to be in a daze, hovering between consciousness and unconsciousness. Lowering his lips to her ears, Aditya whispered, 'Sarala's here.'

Opening her eyes slightly, Neeraja said, 'Go away, please.' Then she called out, 'Thakurpo!' There was no response.

As soon as Sarala approached to touch her feet, Neeraja's body stiffened as though struck by lightning, and her feet jerked away.

'I cannot, I cannot, I cannot give it all away, I cannot,' she uttered hoarsely.

As she spoke, an unnatural power seemed to seize her body; her eyes bulged and began to blaze. She gripped Sarala's hand tightly, her voice became sharper, she screamed, 'There'll be no room for you, you she-devil, no room for you. I'm staying, I'm staying, I'm staying.'

The ashen, emaciated figure in her loose chemise suddenly leapt up from her bed. In a contorted voice she screamed, 'Get out, get out of here this instant, else I'll strike at your heart day after day, I'll suck up all your blood.'

And instantly, she slumped to the floor.

Aditya ran into the room at the sound of her voice. Emptied of life, Neeraja's last words had by then been silenced forever.

Translator's note

> Translating's half poem and half crossword and no doddle.
> Loads of words aren't actual words you can look up, but
> screws of grammar that hold the sentence together. It takes
> yonks to find out what they mean, though once you know
> them you know them.
>
> *Black Swan Green: A Novel*, David Mitchell

THE THREE NOVELLAS in this collection were published in
1901 (*Nashtaneer*), 1933 (*Dui Bon*), and 1934 (*Malancha*).
Although it is not specified, the setting for the first appears to
be the last years of the nineteenth century, while the other are
set in the 1930s against the distant backdrop of the freedom
struggle. Translating them in 2010 poses the challenge of
choice—just what kind of English should be used? Should it
be the English used in conversation in Bengal in the period in
which the novellas are set? Or should it be English as it was
spoken and written in England at that time?

Put another way, should the translation conjecture how
Rabindranath Tagore, who also wrote in English occasionally,
might have written these novellas in English? Or, should the
translations read like original novellas by a different author—
someone who wrote in English and not in Bengali—working
with the same material? The distinction is important, since
the two languages are themselves so fundamentally different

There is a third alternative. It is based on the premise that
any work of fiction is written for contemporary readers, not

necessarily for posterity. For such readers, the language of the fiction was obviously contemporary, whether in 1901 or in 1933 and 1934. Then why not maintain the spirit of contemporary writing even when translating Tagore in 2010? Especially since the modern Bengali that Tagore ushered in remains the Bengali that is in use in much of today's writing too.

Underlying the choices is an even more fundamental question. Should the metaphors, images, and other features of the translation remind the reader that the original was the product of a different culture, employing a different idiom? More simply put, should the translation sound as if it were transposed from another language? Or should it be the content rather than the form that evokes this distance between the reader and the originals, with the translation reading with the fluidity of being composed in English?

The premise of these translations is that the stories themselves provide the historical, social, political, and economic contexts sufficiently; the language of the translations is aimed at capturing the content, register, and nuances of the original, but without creating a deliberate sense of distance in culture, space, and time. The vocabulary and grammar of the translations are modern, but not trendy. Above all there has been an attempt to make the language as close to the tones and registers of English as is possible without compromising the original.

To prevent hiccups while reading, almost everything has been translated from Bengali into an equivalent English, without being retained in the original language in order to maintain a dubious exoticness. The only exceptions are words such as dhoti and kurta whose meaning are easily available and the forms of address used in Bengali families and society, which have been used as alternate 'names' for the characters. For instance, there are specific words for the brother's or cousin's wife (bouthan) or the husband's younger brother or cousin (thakurpo), whose precision is not to be found in English. In *Malancha*, the words 'ayah' and 'knokhi' have been retained. In all cases, a translation has been provided in a footnote in the first instance they are used. A relatively small but intellectually stimulating challenge lies in translating the names of flowers, fruits, and trees—readability rather than clinical accuracy has been the guiding spirit here. On the whole, Tagore is kind to his translators—there are not many local or cultural, social, and political references.

Tagore was a writer of many talents but he was above all a poet. His prose is thus the prose of a poet, filled with highly visual metaphors which are dense with imagery. These have proved to be the greatest challenge in the translation. In many cases only the sense, and not the actual picture or conceit, can be carried over into English. But since a tame translation of meaning alone would not have done justice to the original, images and metaphors more familiar to readers of English have sometimes been used without adding words or phrases not in the original, however. Sometimes the metaphor has been simplified while the image they evoke have been retained.

Here is a literal translation of a section in *Dui Bon*.

> Her vivacity raises ripples in the blood, reaches the heart of the senses, where a solitary string of a golden veena awaits in silence a melody, the melody that makes one resonate with the call of the indescribable.

This is the same passage in translation, keeping the central image of the original intact.

> Her vivacity makes the blood tingle, entering the very core of one's being and bringing the expectant body to life, like the melody that awakens the silent veena.

Here is another example from *Malancha*.

> The scent of the memories of different seasons, mingled with the vapour of Darjeeling tea at dawn, merged with her sighs to raise a storm of mourning in her heart.

It has been translated in the following way.

> She remembered the Darjeeling tea at dawn, whose vapours had carried the aromas of the seasons and now seemed to mingle with her sighs, and felt utterly desolate.

Another of Tagore's stylistic quirks in these novellas is his use of abrupt, short sentences in contrast to the rich, enlarged metaphors. Consider the original opening of *Nashtaneer*.

> Bhupati had no need to work. He had enough money, and, moreover, the land was hot. But the stars at his birth had made him an industrious man. This was why he felt compelled to publish an English newspaper. Now he no longer had to grumble about time hanging heavy on his hands.

Unless it is vital, these translations do not interpret the original text on the reader's behalf, add connecting sentences to to make the prose more fluid, or slip in explanations where more than one reading is possible. The objective has been to maintain, rather than unravel or gloss over, all the ambiguities, hints, and oblique observations that Tagore enriched his prose with—as well as the eccentricities and excesses that sometimes made their presence felt. These translations, in sum, are attempts to be faithful—for better or for worse.

A note on the author

Rabindranath Tagore (1861–1941) was Bengal's most celebrated writer. He won the Nobel Prize for Literature in 1913, becoming the first Indian to win the prize and the only Indian to win it for literature. Regarded by many as a renaissance man, he was a novelist, dramatist, artist, lyricist, educationist, and, above all, a poet.

A note on the translator

ARUNAVA SINHA IS the translator and series editor of the Random House India Classics Series, Bengali. His translations include *Chowringhee* (winner of the Vodafone Crossword Prize for best translation), *My Kind of Girl* (shortlisted for the Vodafone Crossword Prize for best translation), *Middleman*, and *Striker Stopper*.

The Random House India Classics Series aims to publish the great Indian classics in their definitive translations. In the Bengali section, the series will present classic Bengali novels ranging from Peary Chand Mitter's Alaler Gharer Dulal *(1857) to Samaresh Basu's* Mahakaler Rather Ghora *(1977). Many of these books will be translated into English for the first time. Out now, Bankim Chandra Chattopadhyay's* Durgeshnandini.

Λ note on the type

THIS BOOK WAS set in a modern adaptation of a type designed by the first William Caslon (1692–1766). The Caslon face has enjoyed much popularity in modern times. Its characteristics are remarkable regularity and symmetry, and beauty in the shape and proportion of the letters; its general effect is clear and open but not weak or delicate. For uniformity, clearness, and readability it has perhaps never been surpassed.